Young Fluent Readers

Young Fluent Readers

What can they teach us?

MARGARET M. CLARK

Reader in Educational Psychology, University of Strathclyde

HEINEMANN EDUCATIONAL BOOKS
LONDON

Heinemann Educational Books Ltd
48 Charles Street, London W1X 8AH
LONDON EDINBURGH MELBOURNE AUCKLAND EXETER (USA)
HONG KONG SINGAPORE KUALA LUMPUR NEW DELHI IBADAN
LUSAKA NAIROBI JOHANNESBURG KINGSTON PORT OF SPAIN

ISBN 0 435 80220 8

Printed Offset Litho and bound in Great Britain by
Cox & Wyman Ltd, London, Fakenham and Reading
Set in 10/11 pt Baskerville

Contents

List of Tables

LIST OF FIGURES

ILLUSTRATIONS

Preface

In 1970 the present author published the findings of a research into specific reading difficulty based on a community study of 1544 children and follow-up of all those found at 7 years of age to be backward in reading. Children who at 8 years of age were still backward in reading although of average intelligence were studied further. The difficulties of these latter children were found not to be specific to the decoding of print; the finding was rather of a *diversity* of disabilities not an underlying pattern common to this group. There were, in addition, a number of problems in assessing the importance of the particular deficits found in that group of children which appeared to be associated with backwardness in reading.

1. The fact that certain factors are found to be associated with lack of progress does *not* entitle one to assume they are the *cause* of the failure.
2. Some factors, even if causally related to lack of progress, may be so only within certain approaches to learning to read.
3. Those factors which are causally related to learning to read must be distinguished from those which appear so only if the learning takes place in a group situation (see Clark 1970, pp. 131–2).

In order to investigate these three aspects a further study was commenced in 1969, one aspect of which involved using tests similar to those in the earlier study on children commencing school in two particular primary schools with rather different approaches to the teaching of reading. These children have been followed up and their progress in learning to read and spell has been monitored. The results will be reported elsewhere. The study which forms the basis for this present book is an investigation of the aspects listed under 2 and 3 above; namely the extent to which certain characteristics may appear crucial because of the particular approach used in learning to read and the fact that learning to read normally takes place in a group situation – in school.

Thirty-two children who were already reading fluently and with understanding when they started school at approximately five years of age formed the basis for the study – children who were already reading beyond the 'at risk' category in many studies of reading failure. While the earlier study referred to above was a larger-scale community study, this present work is mainly an intensive detailed analysis of the young fluent readers, their strengths, and the weaknesses in spite of which they learned to read early and fluently.

It is hoped that apart from the intrinsic interest of this group of children such a study will lead to greater caution in assuming that certain strengths are essential pre-requisites for success in reading – or equally important, that particular weaknesses inevitably lead to failure.

I am grateful to the Scottish Education Department for an extension of my original grant for a research into children with reading difficulties, which made possible this study of young fluent readers and the related longitudinal study of reading progress; also to the University of Strathclyde which, by permitting me to undertake the research, has carried the hidden costs. I would like to express my particular thanks to Mr J. G. Morris of the Scottish Education Department who has supported this and my related researches in every way.

My thanks are also due to the head teachers and staffs in the schools in Dunbartonshire, Glasgow and Stirlingshire who co-operated throughout in providing access to the children and in completing records of their progress.

This research and the related longitudinal study had a full-time research assistant only briefly and I would like to express my thanks to all those who have helped in any way with the project. I would like to mention particularly Mrs Anne Yelland, Dr Carol Lomax, Mrs Christina Del Priore, Mrs Morag McDonald and Miss Alice Finlay, all of whom were involved in testing at some stage of the study; also Mrs Jane Wye who was responsible for all the final interviews of the fluent readers and the transcription of the parental interviews.

My thanks are due to Mrs Cynthia Forrest who painstakingly typed repeated drafts of the manuscript, and to Heinemann Educational Books for agreeing to publish the research and thus making it available to a wide public.

I appreciate the insights I have gained from contact with the young fluent readers and their parents and hope sincerely that participation in the research has not had adverse effects on any of them.

I would like to record my gratitude to the parents of the fluent readers and to the children themselves without whose continued co-operation this book would not have been possible.

A combination of a lecture by Keith Gardner and a young fluent reader referred by Mrs Helen McLullich stimulated this research; my thanks to them both.

MMC 1976

CHAPTER I

Reading Considered in a Language Context

Trends in Reading Research

Until recently, particularly in psychological research, there has been an emphasis on 'levels of literacy', 'trends in reading standards', on 'backwardness' and 'reading readiness' with little consideration for the processes involved in the development of successful reading. Furthermore the studies have been limited and fragmentary. In the field of literacy levels, for example, criteria for illiteracy, semi-literacy and literacy have been defined in terms of reading ages of under seven years, seven to nine and over nine years. Concern has been shown about the numbers of children who have left school illiterate or semi-literate as so defined. Adequate attention has not, however, been paid to whether a reading age of nine years on this definition and with the available tests, is either a sufficient criterion for literacy, or even gives evidence of a child having acquired the basic skills necessary for reading with understanding the instructional materials and textbooks used in the secondary schools. Studies of trends in reading standards have been directed towards issues such as relative standards between different countries or areas, or variation in standards at different times or under different methods. The recent study in England by Start and Wells (1972) published as *The Trend of Reading Standards*, precipitated the setting up of the enquiry into the teaching of reading and related skills in England and Wales, referred to as the Bullock Committee whose report is entitled *A Language for Life* (D.E.S. 1975). The early chapters of the report are devoted to a discussion of the National Foundation for Educational Research study referred to above and to a consideration of the need for monitoring of national standards with regard to literacy. The remainder of this comprehensive report does, however, emphasize the importance of developing a unified policy for literacy in the school and of ensuring that the oral and written language needs of all children are developed to the full. Again, studies of backwardness in reading have concentrated on children with difficulties, whether general or specific. The strengths of good readers must be considered and also *their deficits* in spite of which they have learned successfully. Only then will there be understanding of which skills are indeed crucial to reading progress.

In the development of reading readiness tests, separate sub-skills have been analysed and tests devised which it was believed would form their basis. Groups of children have been tested and an attempt made to establish which of the tests or groups of tests indicate unreadiness – or are likely to be predictive of failure or children 'at risk'. An extension of such approaches will not further illuminate understanding of the processes in the complex skill of reading. The emphasis is on these instances where children have deficits and fail, but perhaps too little attention is paid to the reasons for the success of the children whose *failure* was predicted by the tests. Relevant in this context is the child described by Krippner (1963) who would clearly have failed some reading readiness tests but at three years of age was already a fluent reader. Only limited help can be expected from studies of reading readiness unless they are considered in a context of the processes involved in, and essential to, reading with under-standing. Even the beginnings of reading represent the 'patterning of complex behaviour' and only when this is appreciated will insight be gained into the factors crucial to reading progress in the early stages (Clay 1972).

Reading in a Language Context

There have been increasing numbers of papers recently in which the emphasis has been on the need to consider reading in a language context. McInnes for example in a paper entitled *Language Pre-Requisites for Reading* discusses the dangers of an emphasis on the technology of reading as a way of improving standards. He claims that the teaching of reading has been increasingly based on the idea that reading 'consists of a bundle of skills' and that publishers have been producing materials aimed at giving practice with these skills.

> The skills orientation is indeed deep rooted. It would seem that if the child's reading growth is to be seen as part of his growth as a person who uses language, then present practices in teaching reading need re-evaluating, modifying and in some cases dis-mantling. (McInnes, 1973, p. 100)

Smith in his much quoted book *Understanding Reading* (1971) stresses the need in teaching reading to consider what the skilled reader can do and the beginning reader is trying to do. In his more recent book *Psycholinguistics and Reading* (1973) he develops this theme further, stressing the need to bear in mind that only a small part of the information necessary for comprehension comes from the printed page. To a great extent Smith in both the above books is dealing with the skills and insights necessary for teaching beginning reading, though what he does is to analyse the features of the skilled reader and consider their relevance for beginning reading. In the recently published manual to their reading scheme entitled *The Written Word*, Reid and Low (1974) consider learning to read and write as kinds of language learning, stressing the need for a bridge from oral to written language. They take account also of what is required for an understanding of the written language of story books, and that of textbooks, beyond the requirements for dealing with the simplified language of the books of the early reading schemes. They stress the need, within the reading scheme, for transition to a language which more nearly approximates the conventions of written language as found in books which have not been explicitly prepared for teaching beginning reading. The views expressed by Reid and Low link well with those of Pearce (1972) who in a recent paper entitled *Literacy Is Not Enough* considers what is involved in understanding the contents of textbooks which children will encounter in the secondary school. Relevant also is a paper by Morris (1973) entitled *You Can't Teach What You Don't Know*, in which she develops the theme of the need of teachers in pre-service training for an understanding of language and an awareness of the relationship between oral and written language, a theme also touched upon by John McInnes in the paper referred to above. These few examples reveal this changing emphasis with an insistence that teachers, even of beginning readers, consider reading and learning to read in a language context.

Oral Language Studies

Although a study of oral language will not reveal how to teach reading, it is important nevertheless to consider the pitfalls into which research into the oral language development of children have fallen and to take account of the variables previously thought to be important and which it is now realized are *not* the crucial variables in delayed language development. Limitation in children's spoken or understanding vocabulary does not seem to be the crucial variable; nor a lack of awareness of syntax, certainly not the ability to use it. Research by Tough (1973a) for example has shown that a careful analysis of even the language of the disadvantaged will reveal a wider use of complex sentence structure than had previously been realized. What is different is the frequency of use of the complex sentence, rather than whether it is used.

Cazden (1971) insists that the important determinant of the oral language elicited from young children is the situation. The topic and the listener are also crucial variables determining the quantity and the complexity of the language produced by children. Thus it is not a question of bombarding children with speech; no more is it a question of attempting to instruct them in the complicated structures of language. The stress should be on interaction between teacher and child in such a way that the need for precision or complexity of language will become apparent as a means towards greater communication.

> If the child is to be helped to discover new meaning for his experiences it will come through those relationships with the teacher which reward his efforts to communicate, since this opens up opportunities for the teacher to extend the child's thinking. (Tough, 1973b, p. 127)

Spoken and Written Language

While it would be quite misleading to regard print as speech written down, it is, nevertheless, important to look at the development of children's oral language and at research in this field in order to determine the starting point in teaching reading. Like Smith (1971) one should deplore the lack of appreciation given to the skills the child brings to the reading task:

> Two things are perhaps surprising about the skills and knowledge that a child brings with him when he is about to learn to read: the sheer quantity and complexity of his ability, and the small credit that he is usually given. (Smith, 1971, p. 223)

It is important to consider not only the extent to which the child is ready for school but also the extent to which the teacher is ready to receive the child *on the level at which he is functioning*. It is also important to realize that almost without exception children do have the visual perception and the auditory discrimination adequate for learning to read. There may be concepts related to these in which they are deficient but not auditory discrimination or visual perception *per se* (Hardy 1973). It is important to define the task of reading as predicting one's way through print and to focus even in the beginning of teaching reading on *anticipation* and *discrimination* rather than identification. The child has to appreciate the crucial discrimination necessary to reading and also what has to be ignored. The language of instruction used by the teacher is also an important aspect whose significance has been highlighted by Reid (1966) and Downing (1969) in their investigations of the extent of understanding of the terms commonly used in reading instruction by children beginning reading. Consideration must also be given to the material used in teaching reading and the extent to which it is leading children to the appropriate strategies; or whether it may on the contrary be such as to force them to use wrong strategies. Last but not least the teacher should be concerned not only with using the appropriate materials and language of instruction, she should also listen to the child both when he is correct *and* when he is wrong. She needs to cultivate the skill of sensitive observation of each child's reading behaviour which will help determine where to proceed in the reading programme for each individual child (Clay 1972). The teacher who regards reading as a communication skill will use a very different approach from the teacher for whom reading is decoding into spoken language. When considering children with reading difficulties, whether they be young or old, it is important to decide the extent to which the difficulties are in effect part of a major and general language problem. Could the backward reader in question understand the text even if it were read to him – if not then surely the problem should not be regarded as specific to reading or as one for which the answer is remedial reading. As with the beginning reader, here also, sensitive observation in the reading situation *and* in other language situations, is crucial.

Oral Reading and its Purposes
It is important to consider the purposes for which children are asked to read orally. It is not sufficient to listen for whether the child's reading is correct or not; nor to correct him when he is wrong. It is equally important to listen to what he says when he is wrong and to ascertain the extent to which he is developing powers of self-correction when alerted to his errors. Some errors (or miscues) form part of the development towards skilled reading – indeed some may be a result of intelligent anticipation, not yet quite precise enough, but nevertheless the beginning of an awareness that print carries a message, that it is a communication in writing (Clay 1969). The purpose for which oral reading by the child is used is important, but also the purposes for which oral reading *to* the child is used. The motivational aspects are frequently stressed and the need for parents and teachers, by reading to children, to make them aware of the enjoyment from books, and so stimulate them to wish to learn to read for themselves. Reading to children not only anticipates the reading

instruction but also is part of the process of learning the characteristics of written language and, therefore, an integral part of the reading instruction. The more the child has become sensitized to the structure of written language the more likely he is to make the appropriate anticipations when reading for himself. Children who have difficulty in learning to read should continue to gain *oral* presentation of progressively more complex written language; otherwise they will be doubly deprived by their limited ability to read for themselves. Attempts to help them to overcome their reading difficulties have perhaps had too limited horizons, and as a result have held back language development by a continued and intensive concentration on the identification of words in isolation, or within simple sentence structures at a time when these children's contemporaries are enjoying the variety, the stimulation and the instruction available with the aid of the range of experiences provided in 'book language' with its own characteristics. Tapes of orally presented *written* language both narrative and instructional are, therefore, an important part of the education of 'remedial' children.

Reading Failure and Language Studies

A too exclusive focus on ways of remedying reading failure may lead to a neglect of two equally important considerations with regard to children with reading difficulties:
1. how to circumvent the restriction of educational experiences which might result from the reading failure, and
2. how to enable such children with reading and associated written language problems to demonstrate adequately the knowledge and skills they have acquired.

This requires an investigation into alternative ways of learning and assessment appropriate to their special needs as well as a consideration of the most effective means of overcoming the reading and associated difficulties. It is therefore important that those involved in remedial education do not become so exclusively preoccupied with the child's needs *within* the remedial context that they overlook the purposes for which the reading skill is required and the sources of education that fluency in, and enjoyment of, reading make possible. One role of the psychologist in relation to remedial education is perhaps in alerting those working with children with difficulties to the developments in research into reading and related skills. One such area of relevance is the consideration of reading in a language context; not just adult reading, or even fluent reading, but all reading being regarded as a communication skill with its own characteristics. Reading considered in a language context would thus have implications not only for the beginning reader but also for the child with difficulties.

The Fluent Reader and the Beginning Reader

Reading instruction, even in the early stages, is gradually coming to be considered in the framework of what the skilled reader can do and the beginning reader is trying to do; so far, however, skilled readers have tended to be equated with adult readers. Even an adult reader does, however, vary his approach and also reveal different levels of competence depending on the type and complexity of print with which he is faced. Indeed one of his skills is just this ability to adapt to the needs of the particular situation. Many attempts have been made to define skilled reading in such a way as to identify its crucial elements and distinguish them from more generalized skills (Maxwell 1974). So far the skilled reader has tended to be equated with the adult reader. It is, however, possible that even a young child, if he is a fluent enough reader, may show some of the characteristics of an adult reader. He may indeed in his response to print have more in common with an adult who is a skilled reader than with his own contemporaries who are less effective.

Early Fluent Readers

A study of young children who are fluent readers might, it was felt, contribute valuable insights into the characteristics of skilled reading. If the focus were to be on those who were already reading fluently when they commenced school it was felt that some additional information might be gained. Such an investigation of young fluent readers might lead to the redressing of the balance from an undue emphasis on strengths or on weaknesses regarded as causally related to progress in reading, but whose importance might indeed be the result of the school environment in which most children learn to read and the framework of expectation within it. The research reported in *Reading Difficulties in Schools* (Clark 1970), commenced when the children in it were seven years of age and while this enabled a study to be made of the incidence of reading difficulty in a school population and of prolonged and severe reading difficulty in children of average intelligence, it was not possible to determine which characteristics of these children were causally related to their reading failure. For such an analysis it would be necessary to commence a study before the children were identified as reading failures. Such a

study is at present under way, that is of children tested on first enter-
ing school and followed through during their attempts at learning to
read. Some of the tests in that study are similar to those which
revealed weaknesses in the backward readers in the earlier study:
thirty-two children who were already fluent readers on starting
school have also been given similar tests. The reading skills of these
fluent readers, their home backgrounds, their school progress and
their results on these psychological tests will be discussed in the
remainder of this book, and the implications of the findings for the
teaching of reading will be considered. Unlike the earlier study of
children with reading difficulties, this is not a community research
but an intensive analysis of selected children who read early; who,
on starting school, were already well beyond the 'at risk' category as
defined in the earlier study, and already at least 'semi-literate' as
defined in official statistics where the criterion is a reading age of
over seven years of age on standard reading tests. A description of
this group of children and of their reading and related attainment at
the time when they were first interviewed will be found in the next
chapter. In the following chapters other information from test results
and details of the children and their families will be discussed. The
history of their development prior to beginning school and in their
early years at school will also be considered. The information
obtained about the children and their families will be presented
mainly in narrative form rather than in tables. Extracts from case
histories will be presented where these give added insights and, in
as far as it is possible to do so, without revealing the identity of the
children.

CHAPTER II

The Fluent Readers and their Attainment on Starting School

The Fluent Readers

In 1969 and 1970 a letter was sent to primary schools in Glasgow and Dunbartonshire, and in 1971 also to schools in Stirlingshire, explaining the purpose of this present research as an attempt to improve the understanding of the processes involved in learning to read by a study of children who were already reading fluently on commencing school. Each school was asked to submit the names of any such children who had recently entered their school. The request to the schools in Dunbartonshire followed almost immediately on the completion of the research referred to in the previous chapter during which the co-operation of all the primary schools in the county had been maintained (*Reading Difficulties in Schools*, Clark 1970). In discussions with the teachers from these schools it had been stressed that there was a need for studies of children from the age of starting school in order to obtain predictive indices of children who were at risk; also for studies of children who had learnt to read prior to the school group-learning situation. Thus, many schools in the county responded either with positive suggestions of possible children for this research, or with regrets at being unable to contribute on this occasion. Schools in Glasgow and Stirlingshire, not involved in the previous research, tended to reply only when offering a possible candidate for the research. In addition to these general requests one selective school was approached directly and this school contributed four children to the study. In this particular school it was a common occurrence for children to be beginning to read, or even reading fluently, on starting school; whereas in some of the other schools the child in this study was the first early fluent reader in the experience of the school.

The fluent readers in this study could, on starting school, already read some books independently, were therefore already well out of the 'at risk' category and were beyond the early books of the beginning reading schemes. Children who were able only to recognize a few words were not included, since the criterion for selection was that a child was able, on initial testing, to read at least twenty-five words on the Schonell Graded Word Reading Test; that is, have a reading age of at least seven years six months on a word recognition test (Schonell 1960). Details of the number of schools who referred children for the study may be seen in Table 1. Several of the schools

Table 1. Details of Schools Referring Fluent Readers

Details	Numbers of schools	Numbers of children
Not included Reading Age 7 yrs 6 mths	7	9
Schools with one child in study	20	20
Schools with two children	4	8
*Schools with four children	1	4
Total included Reading Age equal to or over 7 yrs 6 mths	25	32

* This was a selective school approached directly.

referred children who were included in the study and others able to read, but not at a sufficiently advanced level. All four children referred by the selective school were girls; although this school was co-educational, as were all the schools in the study.

It is not possible from a research study such as this to make an estimate of the numbers of children who begin school already reading fluently, as a screening of school entrants did not form part of the investigation; nor were the children compared with others in the schools who were similar in other respects but not early readers. However, one of the topics discussed with the parents was ways in which these children differed from their brothers and sisters, few of whom had shown the same kind of precocity. A study based on a screening of a large number of schools followed by comparisons between the school progress of the early readers and others of comparable ability who did not read before starting school was beyond the resources of this research. Interesting comparisons can be made between this present study and that by Durkin (*Children Who read Early* 1966) which did include such a comparison. In a surprising number of ways this present group of children were similar to those in Durkin's studies in spite of the fact that hers took place in 1958 and 1961 in the United States with an older age group of children and with a different criterion with regard to reading level.

In the community study referred to earlier (Clark 1970), boys formed the majority of the children of average intelligence with prolonged reading difficulties – fifteen boys and four girls from the original sample of 1544. The majority of those referred as fluent readers on starting school in this study were also boys: twenty boys and twelve girls (four of the latter were from the selective school). An excess of boys is frequently noted in studies of children selected because of extreme deviance in whichever direction and of whatever type. This will be discussed more fully later but it should be noted that the early reading of the boys was more likely to be associated with their other interests, while the girls aimed at extending their reading of stories.

Reading Level

Though some of the children were not referred to the research immediately on starting school all were known to have been reading fluently at that time. Some had started school at under five years of age and others not until about five years six months, depending on their date of birth and the local regulations governing school entry dates. Their ages on initial testing and reading ages on the Schonell Graded Word Reading Test may be seen in Table 2. This test assesses

Table 2. Reading Ages on Schonell Graded Reading Test in Relation to Age at Initial Testing

Age at Initial Testing (in years and months)	7·6–7·11		Frequencies in Reading Ages (in yrs and mths) 8·0–8·11		9·0–9·11		10·0–10·11		11·0–11·11		Totals	
	B	G	B	G	B	G	B	G	B	G	B	G
6·0–6·5	—	—	—	2*	1	1*	—	1	1	—	2	4
5·6–5·11	—	3*	2	1	2	1	3	—	2	—	9	5
5·0–5·5	—	—	2	2*	1	—	4	—	—	—	7	2
Under 5	—	—	2	—	—	—	—	1	—	—	2	1
Totals	—	3	6	5	4	2	7	2	3	—	20	12
	3		11		6		9		3		32	

* Girls from Selective School. B – Boys G – Girls.

ability to read orally words in isolation. The children were subsequently tested on the Neale Analysis of Reading Ability (Neale 1966); a test which consists of a series of six prose passages arranged in order of difficulty. In this test the child's accuracy in reading when assisted by contextual cues is measured; comprehension questions are also asked.[1]

[1] The following passage, which is approximately the level of difficulty

The reading ages of the children on the Neale Analysis ranged from a reading age for accuracy of seven years eight months to eleven years eight months; and for comprehension from six years eight months to twelve years.

Details of these are shown in Table 3.

Table 3. *Reading Ages on Neale Analysis of Reading Ability*

Reading Ages— Comprehension	Reading Ages—Accuracy					
	7+	8+	9+	10+	11+	Totals
12+	—	—	—	—	I	I
11+	—	—	I	—	—	I
10+	—	—	—	—	—	—
9+	—	—	3**	I	I	5
8+	—	1*	5	3	—	9
7+	I	3	6*	2	—	12
6+	I	2	I	—	—	4
Totals	2	6	16	6	2	32

* Girls from Selective School.

Thus all the children were able to meet the requirements of both the Schonell and Neale Reading Tests. With a few of the children any difficulties on the Schonell Test were caused not by reading *per se* but by their unfamiliarity with some of the final words in the test, or by their inability at five years of age to pronounce words such as 'metamorphosis' or 'ineradicable'. They all showed the necessary decoding skill to tackle, without contextual cues to help them, many words which they were unlikely to have met in print, and to give a close approximation to words they were unlikely to have met even in oral language. In their attempts at oral reading where contextual cues were present, as in the Neale Analysis of Reading Ability, these children were clearly making use of such cues, provided the passages were within their level of understanding. While testing them on the Neale Test the author was first alerted to the striking difference between many of these children and others with a comparable read-

---

of the first passage in this test, would have been well within the competence of all those children at the time of starting school.

> A little boy came to see me.
> He left his ball at my house.
> Then he went away.
> Now I play with it myself.
> (from Clark 1970, p. 79)

ing age but who had learned to read in the school-group situation. Most read orally in a manner quite different from the 'precocious' reader who has learned at school and who has had frequent experience of oral reading in a classroom setting. Indeed many seemed to be slowed down by reading orally and perhaps to have their errors increased and comprehension lowered. Further attention will be paid to this point when discussing the early reading experiences of these children; many of whom appear to have read silently even in the early stages.

Spelling Ability

All the children in the sample were tested on the Daniels Spelling Test shortly after starting school (Daniels and Diack 1958). This test consists of forty words ranging from 'on' to 'beautiful' which the child is required to write. Most of the children were able to spell at least twenty of the words when tested which was not necesssarily immediately on starting school but certainly well before any spelling instruction would have commenced in the school. As may be seen from Table 4 only one child had a spelling age of less than six years

Table 4. Spelling Ages on Daniels Spelling Test

Daniels Scores In Spelling Ages No. of Words	Sp. Age	Age on Testing on Spelling Test							
		Under 5		5·0–5·11		6·0–6·11		Totals	
		Boys	Girls	Boys	Girls	Boys	Girls	Boys	Girls
40	12+	—	—	—	—	—	1	—	1
38–39	11+	—	—	1	—	—	—	1	—
36–37	10+	—	—	—	—	—	—	—	—
32–35	9+	—	—	4	—	2	1	6	1
27–31	8+	—	1	5	2	—	1	5	4
18–26	7+	2*	—	5	2	—	1	7	3
9–17	6+	—	—	—	3	—	—	—	3
Up to 8	5+	—	—	1	—	—	—	1	—
Totals		2	1	16	7	2	4	32	

* One boy tired after half the test but subsequently wrote correctly a further 15 of the remaining 20 words.

and his mother commented that he had displayed no interest in writing words, only in reading, prior to starting school. A comparison of their reading and spelling ages is shown in Table 5. Clearly most of these children had started school able not only to identify words in print but also to reproduce letters in a recognizable form and to spell at least regular two and three-letter words correctly. During the parental interviews it was discovered that prior to starting school

Table 5. Comparison of Reading Ages on Neale Analysis and Daniels Spelling Ages

Daniels Spelling Ages	Neale Reading Ages (Accuracy)					Totals
	7+	8+	9+	10+	11+	
12+	—	—	—	1	—	1
11+	—	—	—	—	1	1
10+	—	—	—	—	—	—
9+	—	—	5	1	1	7
8+	—	1	5	3	—	9
7+	1	3	5	1	—	10
6+	1	1	1	—	—	3
5+	—	1	—	—	—	1
Totals	2	6	16	6	2	32

most had shown an interest in writing words as well as in reading. Many children had a blackboard and chalks; these children, how-ever, seemed to have shown particular interest and to have used them for their early attempts at writing words; Durkin also found this interest evidenced by her early readers (Durkin 1966). It seems unlikely that their spelling ability is merely a by-product of their developing skill in reading but rather that it is evidence of a sensi-tivity to the composition of words which is developing from a variety of stimuli in their environment in addition to books. A number of these children used capital letters in their spelling for some or all of the words, possibly because blackboards often have letters printed in capitals while many of the sets of plastic letters which can be pur-chased are in capitals.

Two points are worth making in connection with the spelling test:

(i) The children showed an awareness of the words they did and did not know. In several instances a child made several attempts at a word and was clearly still dissatisfied when he was not able to achieve the correct word. One boy indeed began to cry when asked to write the word 'beautiful' and said he knew he could not write it and asked the tester to write it for him.

(ii) They tended in the errors they did produce in the spelling test to use word forms which were an approximation to English. Some examples of the spelling errors are given below:

any: enee, eny, eni, ani, eany

answer: ansr, anser, ansewr, ansir

fight: fite, fitgh, fiet, fihgt

Although 'beautiful' was naturally too difficult for almost all of them, they either refused to try it, or tended to give a range of interesting approximations: *butfle, buateatfool, butiful, butifol, beutefel* are just some examples.

Errors such as these would gradually be eliminated by further analysis of words together with the application of a limited number of the more basic spelling rules. Meanwhile many of this group of children had a trait which was commendable for the development of good spelling which requires exact recall with one hundred per cent accuracy and not merely recognition as in reading. This characteristic was shown both in their awareness of their errors and in the type of errors they produced. Their sensitivity to the correctness of certain word forms, coupled with a knowledge of their own limitations, would mean, however, that such children might well be reluctant to indulge in free or 'creative' writing should this mean using words they knew they were not yet able to spell correctly. This sensitivity to their own limitations is surely one which should be developed; not discouraged. Yet it is just such a feeling which could result in their becoming discouraged, cramped and limited in the written language they would produce. This could perhaps be prevented if they were to be told the spelling for the necessary words, or encouraged to develop the use of a dictionary to check on words beyond their spelling ability, but which they wished to use. Because of their awareness of plausible alternative spellings – an awareness developed early – they could learn with little difficulty how to use a dictionary for spelling, as they did an encyclopedia for other information. These are both tasks which many children, with less awareness of likely alternatives in English, find difficult. Carefulness, persistence, and a dislike of making mistakes, characteristics of many of these children, are also features commonly found in good spellers (Peters 1970).

In the previous chapter the need for the teacher to observe the child's errors in reading was stressed. It is essential in spelling also to note the errors made by a child and the extent to which they indicate a progressive development of 'miscues' towards an implicit awareness of English spelling patterns. The beginning of such an awareness was clearly to be seen here though some could as yet spell only a limited number of words, and though many would have been quite unable to verbalize the distinctions which were implicit in their behaviour. It seems important not to assume such a lack of awareness because a particular child is unable to verbalize the distinction between such concepts as 'a letter', 'a word', and 'a sentence'. Most of these children were unable to do this at five years of age, yet they did reveal an understanding of their meaning. Ability to explain the meanings of such concepts seemed more related to their home background and the level of sophistication of the language used there rather than to their reading level.

Writing

It is important to bear in mind that within such a group of children, as in any group, there will be a range of levels of motor co-ordination. Not all of the children in the study showed motor co-ordination above average for their age – or indeed average. Thus it was possible to find a child whose spelling ability was superior, as was his reading, but whose co-ordination was very poor. Even several of the children of high intelligence, reading and spelling ability had poor co-ordination. These children, while able to *discriminate* the distinctions between letters and to *recall* them, could not necessarily reproduce them meticulously. In her studies, which were however, with older children, Peters found that speedy and good writing tended to correlate with high spelling ability (Peters 1970). However a high level of motor co-ordination may not be an essential pre-requisite either to the development of reading skill, or indeed spelling ability. It may nevertheless be that within certain school situations a premium is placed on a level of precision of motor co-ordination which is impossible for certain children at such an early stage. The poor motor co-ordination of several of these children caused problems when promotion to a higher class more in keeping with their reading and spelling ability was considered. One parent recently remarked that her son's teacher was amused that a child who could read on such an advanced level was still having difficulty in tying his own laces at seven years of age! Children should none the less be encouraged to write as carefully and clearly as they can so that they have a clear image of the correct spelling of words *in their own writing*. Where they make an error, and know they have done so, they should for the same reason have the opportunity to make the necessary corrections. Some of the children, even though of high ability, were particularly sensitive to the errors they made and would have wished to be allowed to erase them. It seems a pity that this is a practice frowned upon by some teachers. It is important to accept the limitations placed by a child's level of motor co-ordination and, where these are severe, use some technique to ensure that such a child is not thereby doubly penalized.

Premature encouragement of children to write 'creatively' and at length may lead to an unfortunate undervaluing of precision of spelling and of expression. Perhaps while the children are at this early stage in the development of an awareness of what is and is not permissible in printed language, it would be preferable to concentrate on communication using oral language and from that to develop a skill of say, story telling, or story reading from an imaginary book. Many young children when retelling a story which has been read to them, even where they modify the original language, retain the essence of the 'book' language. Children could thus become sensitized to the differences between oral and written language prior to their attempts at reproducing on paper written language for others to read, with all the additional skills this necessitates. Even these advanced children, whose oral language was interesting and whose speech was accurate, seemed reluctant to write at this early stage; a reluctance which was in many ways appropriate to the level of ability they possessed to produce written language of a kind that would satisfy them. In short, even they needed experience of reproducing the language of stories and books, systematic study of the structure of words in the English language and guidance on how to find for themselves the spelling of words they did not know. This sensitive awareness is something which could well be cultivated in more children.

Arithmetic

The arithmetic attainment of these children was formally tested only within the context of the arithmetic sub-test of the Wechsler Pre-School and Primary Intelligence Scale (Wechsler 1967). While the results of the intelligence tests will be discussed in the following chapter, it is worth noting here, however, that this group of children were all making high scores on that sub-test (15·8 Mean S.D. 2·6[1]) and indeed that most of them were still successful with the most difficult items on that test suggesting that their ability was being underestimated by the test. The verbal context in which the questions are posed may have been one reason for their high scores. They also tended to be successful with the items involving money in the

[1] The mean expected is 10 and the standard deviation 3. The *standard deviation* (S.D.) is the measure which indicates the extent to which the scores are clustered around the mean. If the standard deviation is small, scores are concentrated around the mean; if it is large, scores are more widely scattered. If the scores on a test are normally distributed, two-thirds of the scores will lie within one standard deviation on each side of the mean. In comparing the results of tests it is important to take into account both their means and standard deviations.

Stanford Binet Intelligence Test. Unfortunately these items had to be omitted with the later children because of the change to decimalization in the currency which altered their level of difficulty (Terman & Merrill 1961). Several of the children were bored with arithmetic in school and were therefore not necessarily having all their work correct, showing that it is not always true that a child who makes errors needs simpler work! Here, as in spelling which was discussed earlier, it is important to consider the range and type of errors and the consistency with which certain errors appear and whether these indicate a failure to understand that particular process, to learn that specific fact or lack of interest. One of these children was, at the age of five, able to add in his head large numbers which an adult required to write down to check; another, at a slightly later stage, was working out his older sister's sums successfully at home before his mother realized he had not yet been taught that particular process. He had been in trouble in school for taking the wrong sum cards – ones which were harder than those he was expected to do.

Thus even when first studied on starting school, the level and range of attainments of these children was considerable; in few was the attainment confined to the reading situation. Already on their initial visit to the university it was clear how ready and eager they were to learn from all new experiences. The range of attainments, motivation, powers of concentration and attention to detail shown by these children make it important to analyse both their characteristics *and* the environment within which they had developed in this way. Before discussing the family background of the children and comparing them with their siblings, the results of the intelligence and other psychological tests which were given at the initial interviews will be presented in the following chapter.

CHAPTER III

Assessment of Intelligence and Other Characteristics

It was clearly of importance to make some estimate of the intellectual level of the fluent readers and of their abilities on a range of psychological tests whose content is regarded as relevant to the development of reading skills. As had been anticipated a number of the children were highly intelligent as measured by the tests, although this was not true of all the group. What was felt to be of particular interest was the kind of test on which they were successful; these they enjoyed doing and those they regarded as so simple that they were hardly worthy of the effort – which was true of several tasks which normally cause some difficulty to children of their age. All those involved during the many hours devoted to the psychological assessment of the children, at a time when the children had only recently started school, were impressed by their enthusiasm, particularly for the more intellectually challenging tasks, by their ability to sustain concentration over the long period necessary for the extensive programme of testing, and also by their ease in relating to strange adults in a variety of situations.

Intelligence

In a number of the studies of precocious children including the classical studies by Terman and his colleagues (Terman 1925) a version of what is now known as the Stanford Binet Intelligence Scale has been the basic measure of intelligence. Even in the newer revisions of the Stanford Binet Intelligence Scale, however, this test has a structure such that children may be assessed on quite different sub-tests even if they are of the same actual, or the same mental age (Terman and Merrill 1961). As a result, apart from the global intelligence quotient, it is difficult to make other than qualitative comparisons. The Wechsler Intelligence Scale for Children, in contrast, has separate verbal and performance scales, and within each of these, all five sub-tests are presented to all children whatever their actual or mental age (Wechsler 1949). This is one reason why the test has been favoured in recent studies of reading difficulties where Full Scale Intelligence Quotient, verbal/performance discrepancies and sub-test profiles have been considered (See Belmont and Birch 1966 for a discussion of a number of such studies and more recently

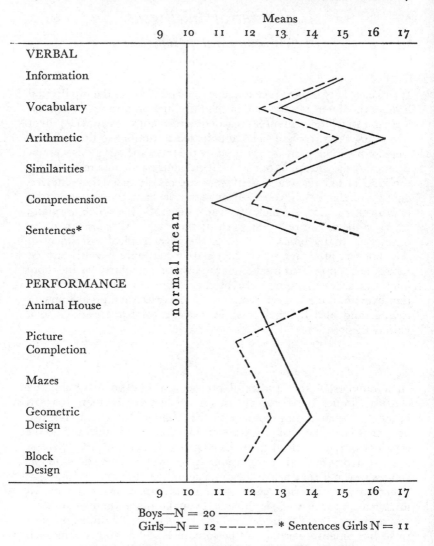

Figure 1. Mean Scores on WPPSI Sub-tests for 32 Fluent Readers

Clark 1970, Rutter, Tizard and Whitmore 1970 and Naidoo 1972). In their report on the preparation of a Scottish Standardization of the WISC the Scottish Council for Research in Education warned on the inappropriateness of the use of WISC for sub-test analysis with children under eight years of age even though the norms for the test are available from five to sixteen years of age (SCRE 1967). Fortunately there is now a downward extension of the WISC, namely the Wechsler Pre-School and Primary Scale of Intelligence covering the age range four to six-and-a-half years which has been used in this present study (Wechsler 1967). Several of the sub-tests of the WISC were considered inappropriate for the younger children and new sub-tests were therefore substituted in the WPPSI:

Picture Arrangement in the WISC is replaced by Geometric Designs in the WPPSI;
Coding in WISC by Animal House in WPPSI;
Object Assembly is replaced by Mazes which is a supplementary test in WISC.

In the other sub-tests WPPSI items are a downward extension and in most instances the final items are from the WISC. Unfortunately 'Coding' and 'Picture Arrangement', two of the tests which do not feature in WPPSI, are two of the sub-tests on which much of the attention to deficiencies in children with reading difficulties has been focused.

The range of test results in the WPPSI with this group of fluent readers was as follows:

Full Scale   IQ Range 98–146 Mean 122·5 SD 11·9
Verbal   IQ Range 100–155 Mean 122·2 SD 14·2
Performance IQ Range 95–134 Mean 118·4 SD 10·0

As may be seen from the sub-test profile in Figure 1 the pattern of scores for the boys and girls is very similar and all sub-test means for the scaled scores are above average. The mean score for Arithmetic is particularly high: 15·8 S.D. 2·6, and no child had a score below average (which is ten). The IQs were calculated on the scores of the ten basic sub-tests but the supplementary 'sentences' test was given to all but one of the children. The children found this memory for sentences a simple test and also all scored average or above on that test.

The verbal/performance discrepancies of the children in this study are shown in Table 6. In the author's study of children with reading difficulties 58·3 per cent of the sample of 230 backward readers obtained WISC verbal/performance discrepancies of less than ten

Table 6. *Difference between Verbal and Performance IQs on WPPSI*

	Discrepancy in Points	Frequencies Boys	Girls	Totals	
	35–39	1	—	1	
	25–34	—	—	—	
Verbal IQ Higher	20–24	2	2	4	} 25%
	15–19	1	—	1	
	10–14	1	1	2	
+	1–9	5	5	10	
Verbal & Perf. IQ Same	0	1	—	1	} 62·5%
–	1–9	7	2	9	
Performance IQ Higher	10–14	1	2	3	} 12·5%
	15–19	1	—	1	
Totals		20	12	32	

points which is very similar to the result obtained here on the WPPSI with 62·5 per cent of this sample obtaining such a result. In the present study, however, the larger discrepancies tended to be in favour of a higher verbal score – 25 per cent had a discrepancy of more than ten points in that direction with five of the children having a discrepancy of twenty or more points in that direction. In the study of poor readers, on the contrary, the tendency was for the performance IQ to be higher.

Although at first sight it appears that use of the Wechsler Tests provides a comprehensive scale for analysis of intellectual functioning from pre-school to adulthood there is a weak link around six to seven years of age, which in Britain is often a crucial age for assessment. This weakness became evident when testing the brighter children in this study. While they were still within the range for the norms of the WPPSI, they were in actual fact reaching the ceiling on a number of the sub-tests. Several children could have obtained the same final scaled scores or even the same IQ with a much lower level of functioning. One child gave a selection of definitions on most of the words, any one of which might have justified the two point score. For this reason it was decided to retest on the Stanford Binet Intelligence Scale in order to determine their ceiling on a language-based test and to make it possible to compare them with the various groups identified in earlier studies as gifted. In Table 7 the results on WPPSI and Stanford Binet Tests are shown. Most of these children obtained higher IQs on the Stanford Binet than the WPPSI.

Table 7. *Comparison of Intelligence Scores as Measured on WPPSI and Stanford-Binet Intelligence Scales*

Stanford Binet Freq. at Each IQ Level	WPPSI Frequencies at Each IQ Level						Totals
	90+	100+	110+	120+	130+	140+	
170+	—	—	—	—	2	1	3
160+	—	—	—	—	1	1	2
150+	—	—	1	2	1	—	4
140+	—	—	6	2	4	—	12
130+	—	3	1	1	—	—	5
120+	1	1	1	—	1	—	4
110+	—	—	1	1	—	—	2
100+	—	—	—	—	—	—	—
Totals	1	4	10	6	9	2	32

Twenty-one had IQs of 140 or more on the Stanford Binet, the level at which 'giftedness' was defined in Terman's studies of giftedness; while several were in the sub-group singled out for special study by Terman (viz. IQ 170+). As was mentioned earlier it is difficult to make quantitative comparisons on the performance of the children within the Stanford Binet as a child's performance on one group of tests determines the particular sub-tests to be administered at each successive level. It was noticeable, however, that the successes were frequently in tests involving memory for language such as 'digits' (Year X), digits reversed (Year IX), 'naming the days of the week' (Year VIII) which was passed by thirty of the children, 'memory for sentences' and also 'rhymes'. In short, most of this group of children who were already able to read when they started school were found to be of above average intelligence and on the Stanford Binet Intelligence Test most scored at a level at least two years in advance of their actual age.

It is easy to dismiss these children, to say that many of them are 'gifted', as some certainly are, as measured by an intelligence test; and to regard their achievements as irrelevant to the understanding of the development of reading skills in other more 'normal' children. Already, however, intelligence tests are being questioned as measures of innate ability and the extent to which they are a combination of innate potential and environmental enrichment must be considered. Indeed, the Stanford Binet Intelligence Test is being used in some pre-school intervention studies, not only as a baseline assessment, but also to measure the effectiveness of the programme. There has been a trend away from accepting the results of the Stanford Binet test as a measure of innate potential and predictor of future level of functioning as had previously been accepted; though, perhaps, with certain reservations, when predictions were based on the testing of pre-school children. It was shown in various classical studies that under favourable circumstances the measured IQ of pre-school children could be greatly increased and with this came the realization that the lack of success in predicting future IQ from early assessments of intelligence required some more fundamental explanation than had previously been given (Hunt 1961). Following the wave of optimism about the possibilities of dramatic changes in IQ as a result of intervention programmes there has been a reappraisal of the other features apart from changes in basic level of functioning which might contribute to, or even explain, this rise in test results. Significant in this context is the study by Zigler and Butterfield (1968) on the effect of test conditions and the interaction of this with nursery-school attendance in influencing results; also the differential effect of length of time taken to administer an intelligence test (see Cazden in *Language and Poverty*, Williams 1970).

More recently Stanley in *Compensatory Education for Children Ages 2 to 8* (1973) has commented:

> This is not to say that any child was coached on Stanford-Binet materials, but instead that one-to-one relationships with adults in pre-school programmes seems almost certain to make young children function more willingly and effectively when with an individual mental tester than they do initially when tested 'cold'. (Page 5).

With these fluent readers the intellectual stimulation of the tests was itself rapport-making and the skill of the tester was required only in maintaining and matching the child's high level of functioning rather than in stimulating it.

While certainly not wishing to decry the level of functioning of this group of children, nor to suggest that the results are entirely an artefact of the testing situation, it would be equally mistaken to use it as *the* explanation for their fluent early reading. It is important not to dismiss either their advanced language and intellectual development, or their development of reading skills and interest in reading, as the result of specific identified skills or of innate potential, but to consider the characteristics of their environment which, *interacting with* their potential skills, have assisted this precocious development. It seems more appropriate in the light of recent researches in this area, the present results on the psychological measures, and the communication skills shown by the children in a variety of situations, to consider their early reading as one offshoot of their developing language skill. It is, in short, one of the ways in which these children extend their experiences. The reasons for these comments will become clearer in the light of discussion of their family background and the development of their brothers and sisters. In many instances they also showed communication skills and language interaction patterns similar to those being stressed here and also, later success in school, although they were not fluent in reading at the pre-school stage.

Language and Related Skills

The Illinois Test of Psycholinguistic Abilities (ITPA) was used in the author's earlier study of children with reading difficulties (Clark 1970), the edition of ITPA, which is a measure of various aspects of language development, which was available at that time was, however, the experimental edition (McCarthy and Kirk 1961). The sixty-nine children tested on the ITPA were those who were backward in reading when eight years of age but of average intelligence (at least one IQ on WISC 90 or above). These children were found to have mean language ages well below their actual ages. Disappointingly little discrimination based on sub-test analysis was found for the group as a whole, in spite of claims that the ITPA is a valuable diagnostic tool in planning remediation; it was still possible that individual children's profiles might have provided leads towards such programmes, an aspect which was not studied in detail in that particular study. A number of weaknesses were noted in the test, some concerning its use with British children, others of more general concern. A revised edition is now available which is greatly improved in many ways, and has simpler terminology; this edition has an additional sub-test and two supplementary tests.

The ten basic sub-tests of the revised edition were used in the present study. In the manual it is advised that scaled scores are used in any analysis of results rather than psycholinguistic ages (Kirk, McCarthy and Kirk 1968). These scaled scores make it possible to make comparisons across age groups as they are transformations of raw scores such that at each age for each test the mean performance should be 36 with a standard deviation of 6.

The overall mean-scaled scores for both boys and girls in this group of fluent readers were slightly above average but still no more than six points, or one standard deviation above the expected mean (boys Mean S.S. 41·8, S.D. 3·4; girls Mean S.S. 41·4, S.D. 2·9). On only four of the sub-tests were the mean scores more than six points above the expected mean. It is also interesting to note the similarity of results for the boys and girls (see Table 8).

Table 8. Scales Scores on ITPA Sub-tests

| | Boys | | Girls | |
	Mean*	S.D.*	Mean*	S.D.*
Auditory Vocal Tests				
Auditory Reception	40·8	8·4	43·3	5·5
Auditory Association	45·0	7·4	45·0	7·1
Verbal Expression	36·1	4·3	36·8	4·6
Auditory Sequential Memory	51·8	6·4	43·4	8·6
Grammatic Closure	56·0	6·1	55·3	5·4
Visual Motor Tests				
Visual Reception	36·2	5·4	36·8	4·7
Visual Association	36·5	8·2	38·9	6·6
Manual Expression	37·2	7·2	36·3	5·6
Visual Closure	35·6	6·0	37·3	5·7
Visual Sequential Memory	42·8	7·0	42·8	4·4
Overall Mean	41·8	3·4	41·4	2·9
Number	20		12	

* Mean Scaled Score expected for each sub-test is 36 and Standard Deviation 6.

It has been argued that in addition to knowing a child's intellectual ability and achievement level a teacher needs information on the appropriate remediation to correct a child's reading disability.

The dissatisfaction with classification instruments has led to the recent development of tests for specific functions that give clues to remediation. The Illinois Test of Psycholinguistic Abilities (ITPA), the subject of this report represents an effort along these lines. (Paraskevopoulos and Kirk, 1969, p. 5)

A comparison between the results of this group of young fluent readers aged about six years when tested and the backward readers of average intelligence tested at about nine years of age on the experimental edition is striking not for the differences in the profiles but for their similarity. This is all the more surprising because of the differences in age, scoring and edition of the test used. Although the fluent readers were scoring generally at or above average and the backward readers were scoring below average both groups were higher on the tests involving auditory than those involving visual input. In Figure 2 the profiles for boys and girls in both studies are shown for comparison. The terminology is different in the two editions but the sub-tests have been numbered to correspond. The mean

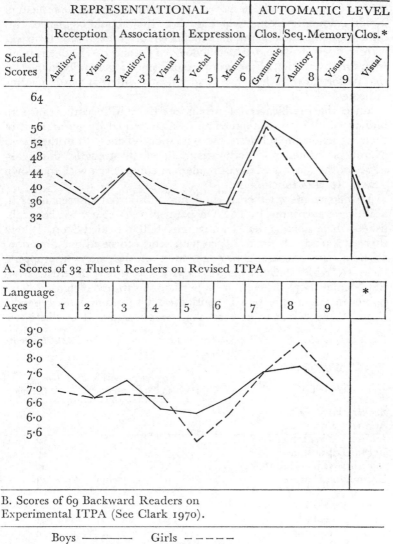

Scaled Scores	REPRESENTATIONAL						AUTOMATIC LEVEL			
	Reception		Association		Expression		Clos.	Seq. Memory		Clos.*
	Auditory 1	Visual 2	Auditory 3	Visual 4	Verbal 5	Manual 6	Grammatic 7	Auditory 8	Visual 9	Visual
64										
56										
52										
48										
44										
40										
36										
32										
0										

A. Scores of 32 Fluent Readers on Revised ITPA

Language Ages	1	2	3	4	5	6	7	8	9	*
9·0										
8·6										
8·0										
7·6										
7·0										
6·6										
6·0										
5·6										

B. Scores of 69 Backward Readers on
Experimental ITPA (See Clark 1970).

Boys ———— Girls – – – – –

A.   Boys N = 20   Girls   N = 12
B.   Boys N = 46   Girls   N = 23
* Visual Closure Sub-test is not in Experimental Edition

*Figure 2. Comparison of Mean Sub-test Scores of the Fluent Readers aged 5–6 years of age
and Backward Readers aged 8 years of age.*

scores on the Visual Closure test, which did not appear in the experimental edition, have been moved to the end of the profile instead of beside grammatic closure which is where they should be placed. It is difficult to feel that any prediction of necessary remediation for backward readers or strengths specific to good readers can be determined from an observation of the group results since a generally high relative performance rather than a specifically different pattern seems indicated.

Since the significance of results on the ITPA with regard to individual children is claimed to be determined by an analysis of their scores on the sub-tests and deviations of these from their own overall performance, a study was made of the strengths and weaknesses of the individual fluent readers in comparison with their own general level of functioning.

To determine whether a child has substantial discrepancies in abilities as measured by ITPA a point of reference must be established which may be the Mean or the Median Scaled Score. Where there is a tendency for the discrepant scores to be in one direction, as here, the Median is recommended as the more appropriate measure (Kirk, McCarthy and Kirk, 1968, p. 95). A difference from the Median Scaled Score on a particular sub-test of ten or more points in either direction is considered a substantial discrepancy. From Table 9 it may be seen that twenty-nine out of thirty-two

Table 9. Discrepancies on ITPA Sub-tests in Relation to Each Child's Own Median Scaled Score

| | Frequencies of Children Scoring | | |
	Below*	Above*	At Ceiling
Auditory Vocal Tests			
Auditory Reception	2	2	3
Auditory Association	0	7	2
Verbal Expression	3	0	0
Auditory Sequential Memory	1	17	20
Grammatic Closure	0	29	14
Visual Motor Tests			
Visual Reception	7	0	1
Visual Association	5	0	0
Manual Expression	4	0	1
Visual Closure	3	0	0
Visual Sequential Memory	1	3	6

* Number of children (out of 32) scoring above or below their own Median Scaled Score by ten or more points.

fluent readers had a Scaled Score for Grammatic Closure ten or more points above their own Median Scaled Scores; seventeen had such a discrepancy in Auditory Sequential Memory. A number of children had already reached the ceiling in some of the sub-tests although the oldest child at the time of testing was only six years eight months and the norms for the revised version of ITPA used here extend to ten years three months. Twenty children were already at the ceiling in Auditory Sequential Memory and fourteen in Grammatic Closure.

Thus, although these children appeared well above average on the ITPA, an analysis of the sub-tests on which they were successful as a group revealed that these were tests involving auditory rather than visual input, indeed on a number of the tasks involving visual input which on this test is not however of print, half of the group were functioning at a level *below* their age on testing. The sub-tests on which this group were outstanding were *Auditory Sequential Memory* (memory for digits), *Grammatic Closure* which involves successful completion of sentences such as 'Here is a bed. Here are two . . .', and to a lesser extent *Auditory Association* which involves completion of sentences such as 'Grass is green. Sugar is . . .'

These results are in line with the findings on the Stanford Binet and Wechsler Intelligence Scales, supporting the view that although other aspects may be above average in some of the children, auditory memory for sounds in sequence, and tasks involving completion in a language context are the areas in which the group as a whole appear to be particularly successful. It is not possible to determine whether, or to what extent, the success in these sub-tests caused, or resulted from, their early success in reading. What is clear, however, is that outstanding success in some of the other sub-tests was neither a cause of, nor caused by their reading progress. The three tests involving visual input (visual reception, visual association, visual closure) were not areas of strength in this group. Reading to children, especially where this involves frequent repetition of the same stories, may well lead to improved ability to predict one's way through print by anticipating the correct word or possible correct words. When, as in this group, this is combined with the ability to read for themselves with understanding it may well be that the sensitive awareness of the appropriate words in context results from, rather than explains, their reading success – or at least that they are inter-related. Thus the results of the ITPA added little of diagnostic value on the fluent readers when taken in association with their already known scores on the other language tests – and when compared with profiles of children known to have had prolonged reading difficulties. They do, however, suggest the need for even greater caution in planning remediation programmes based on deficits shown on such tests. It may be that the best way to improve scores on the sub-tests on which these children excelled is to practise reading! Where the child cannot read for himself there may be a place for a wide experience of written language presented in oral form with encouragement to the child to predict sequences and to learn to anticipate in a language context. Ability to process visual material unrelated to the printed word was certainly not shown to be a strength of these children – either causing or caused by their reading success.

Visuo-Motor Tests

The fluent readers were also given the Bender Visual Motor Gestalt Test (Bender 1946) which was scored as in the study of children with reading difficulties according to the Koppitz scoring system which has been used in a number of studies of school progress (Koppitz 1964). The test has been used as one of the predictors of reading failure both when administered individually and also with group administration, where there is a single large copy of the designs to be reproduced, or where each child has his own copy. Some problems in the use of the Koppitz scoring have been reported by Broadhurst and Phillips (1969); while the present author in an unpublished longitudinal study of children first tested on starting school at five years of age also found difficulties with use of the test with such young children. The type of errors which are regarded as significant with regard to school progress and included in the scoring system are rotation of designs and incorrect placing of the parts in relation to each other, rather than errors of precision caused by poor motor co-ordination. Since the scoring is on an error system, in order to score the test it must be possible to distinguish the separate parts in the child's attempts at a design. Thus, if the child draws well and clearly, faithfully reproducing the design, as did some of the fluent readers, he will obtain a low error score. As the number of errors increases so will the error score, but only until a point when a design is too badly drawn for the variety of errors to be distinguishable. Thus where a young child with poor motor co-ordination attempts the task he may have a certain number of distinguishable errors but in addition a number of unscorable designs as had four children in this study.

The error scores of the fluent readers in relation to their reading ages are shown in Table 10. Because of the difficulty found by some children in this study, and in the longitudinal study, in reproducing the drawings and the view of the present author that ability to

Table 10. Bender Error Scores in Relation to Reading Age on Schonell Reading Test

Reading Ages	0	1	2	3	4	5	6	7	8	9	10	Total
11+	—	—	1	—	—	—	1*	1	—	—	—	3
10+	—	—	2	—	4**	2	—	—	—	1	—	9
9+	—	1	1	1	1	—	—	1	—	1	—	6
8+	—	—	—	1	2	1	1	2*	—	2	2	11
7+	—	—	—	—	—	—	1	—	—	1	1	3
Total	—	1	4	2	7	3	3	4	—	5	3	32

Koppitz Age 5–0 to 5–5 expected Mean Error Score 13·6 S.D. 3·6
5–6 to 5–11 „ „ „ „ 9·8 S.D. 3·7
6–0 to 6–11 „ „ „ „ 8·5 S.D. 4·1
* Four children had unscorable designs.

discriminate between designs similar in all but position might be more important to reading progress than ability to *reproduce* designs in the correct orientation, two supplementary tests were devised using 'Bender type' design and letter-like forms. In the first test the child had to indicate which of four designs differing in rotation was identical in position to a sample card, after a demonstration item in which the importance of position had been stressed. In the second test the child was first shown a design then after it had been withdrawn he had to indicate which of the four on the card was identical in position. Both these tests were given to the fluent readers and to the larger sample in the longitudinal study. It will therefore be possible to check which of the children, while having unscorable Bender results or high error scores, were able, when their attention was drawn to the importance of position, to match the appropriate designs. It was felt that the first supplementary test requiring matching might be associated with reading progress, while the second involving immediate memory might have some connection with spelling. These hypotheses will be tested on the larger scale study. It was certainly true that on the initial Bender Test even some of the fluent readers with high reading ages made high error scores, although few had excessively high scores compared to that expected for their age group. On the matching task on 'Bender type' designs, twenty-two of the fluent readers made no errors on the twelve items, seven made one error and the remaining three made only two errors. Even the youngest found this a simple task which they performed quickly with a minimum of errors. The second supplementary test involving immediate memory caused difficulty for a number of the children (although the designs were similar); half the group made no more than two errors. Several children had, however, few items correct; even some of the good readers. It was also noticeable that several of the children lost interest in the task very quickly.

Taken in isolation, these results cannot be regarded as important. However, in conjunction with the results on the ITPA visual sub-tests they do seem to reinforce the view that although some good readers may have good visuo-motor co-ordination or have a good memory for visually distinguishing features in designs, it is possible for even young children to become very fluent readers in spite of an average or below average ability to reproduce or even to remember in their correct orientation isolated designs sufficiently clearly to identify them from a range of alternatives.

In the following chapter the results of the fluent readers on a test of auditory discrimination will be discussed in rather more detail since it seemed clear that although on the particular test used the fluent readers made few errors, the language context in which the test is administered might be an important contributor to their success.

CHAPTER IV

Auditory Discrimination and What Else?

Tests of Auditory Discrimination

Tests such as Wepman's Auditory Discrimination Test (Wepman 1958) are being used clinically with children who show reading problems in order to identify their areas of difficulty with a view to planning appropriate remediation. Similar items are also appearing in reading readiness batteries for school beginners in an attempt to identify 'at risk' groups. According to Wepman 'The task presented to the child is a simple one. It measures only the ability to hear accurately' (Manual for Wepman Test 1958). The child is asked to listen to pairs of words read to him and to identify whether a single word is repeated or whether the pair consists of two different words. It is stated in the manual that 'the test has been found useful in selecting children, especially those in early elementary school years, who are slower than their peers in developing auditory discrimination'. It is also stated that this ability is related to speech accuracy and to reading ability and that the administration of the test to older five-year-olds and younger six-year-olds will indicate those who are likely to have difficulty learning to use the phonics needed for reading.

The test consists of forty items, in thirty there are two different words in a pair; in the remaining ten pairs the same word is said twice, the results being interpreted as follows:

(a) if the child makes more than three errors on the ten identical pairs the score is regarded as invalid;

(b) if he makes more than fifteen errors on the pairs which are different the score is regarded as invalid;

(c) if he makes up to fifteen errors by failing to distinguish the pairs which are different, the score is interpreted as reflecting poor auditory discrimination according to the following criteria:

> For 5-year-olds greater than 6 errors
> For 6-year-olds greater than 5 errors
> For 7-year-olds greater than 4 errors
> For 8-year-olds greater than 3 errors

Auditory Discrimination of the Fluent Readers

When the auditory discrimination of the thirty-two fluent readers was assessed on the Wepman Test, the children were between five and six years of age. The following results were obtained:

(i) None of the children had scores which were invalid because of failure to distinguish the ten identical pairs. One made two errors in the ten items; three made one error and the remaining twenty-eight made no errors.

(ii) No child had a score which was regarded as invalid because of more than fifteen errors on the word pairs which were different. Indeed the highest score was seven errors.

(iii) Only three children had six or more errors (two girls and a boy). Their reading ages were seven years eight months, eight years four months and eight years eleven months when tested initially on the Schonell Graded Word Reading Test, and the oldest was only six years of age when tested on the Wepman Auditory Discrimination Test.

Clearly even at this very early age, auditory discrimination was not a problem for these children. They quickly grasped the nature of the task and answered without hesitation. The test was very quickly completed with no problems of motivation or lack of concentration. It is significant that the most common errors involved the following word pairs: fie-thigh (24), sheaf-sheath (21), clothe-clove (15), vow-thou (14) – all involving the discrimination of 'th' (the number of children making the error is shown in brackets). Apart from this, few children had any difficulty with word pairs where the difference was in the initial phoneme – pairs such as pork-cork (2), gum-dumb (2). Errors tended to be in pairs where the difference was in the medial vowel or the ending although the thirty items are made up as follows: difference in beginning 13; medial vowel 4, difference in ending 13.

There are a number of important points to be made, however, in connection with this test and the task it represents for the child. Not only do these children appear to have good auditory discrimination but, equally important, all have the following characteristics:

(i) They quickly grasp the nature of a task such as this, that is they have the *cognitive skills* to handle the situation.

(ii) They enjoy word games and therefore they are *interested* to 'play the game' which is how they perceive a task such as this – not as a 'test' by a strange adult. As one child said, 'Oh you mean words that rhyme' (that was at five years of age).

(iii) They have the *motivation* to sustain concentration on a task for a lengthy period of time without being distracted by extraneous noises or strange surroundings.

(iv) They all have *clear articulation* themselves which is mentioned by Wepman in the manual as associated with success in this test.

(v) Most of them have an *extensive vocabulary* and thus many of the words to be discriminated are within their comprehension (see above for the word pairs which did cause difficulty).

(vi) Last, but certainly not least, they can all read and therefore, young as they are, they are fully aware of the *significance of the task* – discrimination between like-sounding words has been an aspect of the development of their reading skill.

Auditory Discrimination of an Unselected Group of Children

Brief reference to the contrasted results from a parallel study of three successive intakes of children starting in two primary schools who were also tested on the Wepman Test between five and six years of age is relevant in order to emphasize the skills which *in addition to* auditory discrimination, seem to be required for success in this test. The results on the Wepman Test for the total group of 197 children aged five to six years of age were as follows:

Invalid score on identical word pairs 24 children
   (error score greater than 3)
Invalid score on different word pairs 22 children
   (error score greater than 15)
Poor auditory discrimination 70 children
   (error score 6–15)
(In contrast none of the fluent readers had invalid scores)

Thus in that group of 197 children only 81 children had valid scores on both scales and were assessed by this test as having good auditory discrimination while 58·9 per cent had invalid scores or poor auditory discrimination. All 197 children who started in either of two schools in 1970, 1971, and 1972 respectively are being followed up and their later progress in reading and spelling is being assessed (this study will be reported elsewhere). It is clear already, however, that while children with low error scores on the Wepman Test tend after two years at school to have progressed in reading, the converse is not necessarily true; that is, children with *high* error scores or invalid results on the Wepman may, or may not, have low scores on subsequent reading tests. It should be noted that the teachers in the study were not alerted to the children's auditory discrimination results as this might have influenced their treatment of the children in the classroom situation during the research.

An analysis was made of the word pairs in the Wepman Test which caused the greatest difficulty in discrimination. The following are some of the word pairs which children with valid scores claimed to be the same and the percentage making each error:

fie – thigh	69·5 per cent	dim – din 49·0 per cent
vow – thou	62·3 per cent	shoal – shawl 41·7 per cent
sheaf – sheath	60·9 per cent	

Here, as with the fluent readers, the words causing difficulty required either a discrimination of 'th' from 'v' or 'f' or had a difference in the ending or the medial vowel. The error rate was however much higher than for the fluent readers all of whom had valid scores according to Wepman's criteria.

It is noteworthy that although articulation difficulty with the 'th' sound is common in boys until as late as seven years of age, the children in this group of fluent readers already spoke clearly with few articulatory difficulties even when starting school which was not true of the unselected group (see Templin 1957 and Hardy 1973). Further, as may be seen from the word pairs listed above, a number of the words in the Wepman Test resulting in high error scores are beyond the comprehension of most children aged five to six years of age – particularly of children from the background typical of a high proportion of poor readers. Indeed some of the word pairs which gave problems even to the fluent readers were unusual enough to be known to only a few of them. The problem in devising items for a test such as the Wepman is that in order to meet the strict criteria with regard to position and type of discrimination it is necessary to use some word pairs which are less familiar than might have been desirable. The failure of many children to discriminate the word pair 'bum – bomb' may have been because of the unexpectedness of the word 'bum' in this context, which could have led the child to fail to attend to the next word. The word 'bum' is one which a child in Scotland would not expect to hear from an adult in polite society, being a slang word for 'posterior', whereas in America, where the test was devised, this is a common expression with a different meaning! Should this explanation be true, the error rate might drop were this word pair reversed and yet 'bomb – bum' is still the same discrimination of sounds.

An Alternative Measure of Auditory Discrimination

Because of the large numbers obtaining invalid scores or high error scores and the suspicion that the nature of the test might contribute to this, it was decided to administer a further test to the children in the unselected group, devised in such a way that:

(a) the words were likely to be familiar to the children in this age group, that is the *vocabulary* was simplified.

(b) the words could be represented pictorially so that the task was not to identify the pairs as 'same' or 'different' but to indicate on a card with drawings of a 'cap' and a 'cup' for example, which word the tester was saying, thus the *response* was simplified; and

(c) although, as on the Wepman Test, the child was not allowed to look at the tester, the child had in this test, pairs of drawings to study – thus *concentration* was improved;

(d) although the test contained forty items, the time required to administer the test, even to children under five years of age, was much reduced since the instructions were quickly understood and responses given speedily – this resulted in much improved *motivation*.

The words were selected from the pairs listed by Templin; selection being based on choice of words which could be represented pictorially and which were most likely to be known to Scottish children (Templin 1957, p. 159). Both words of a pair were said to the child followed by only *one* of the words, whereupon the child had to point to the appropriate picture. With the same unselected group of 197 children tested at around five years of age – that is six months earlier than on the Wepman the following results were obtained:

(i) No child failed to understand the task.

(ii) No child obtained an error score of more than twenty.

(iii) Only 36 children had more than six errors in the forty items.

(iv) 50 children who obtained two errors or less on this test obtained invalid scores on the Wepman Test or appeared to have poor auditory discrimination.

Similar types of discrimination to those in the Wepman Test did, however, give cause for difficulty (for example, mouse – mouth; bag – back; ship – chip; cap – cup) the errors being mainly on pairs differing in ending or medial vowel.

Implications of the Results

The simplified task was not administered to the fluent readers because none of them had any problems with the Wepman test. It is important nevertheless to quote these results in order to emphasize the point that it was to some extent the *complexity of the task* presented in the Wepman test which led to the difficulties of many of the unselected group and the comparative success of the fluent readers.

Two quotations from those who have questioned the implications of results of tests such as the Wepman are perhaps relevant:

> By the time children complete grade one, then, it appears that they experience very few phoneme discrimination difficulties, at the level of the individual phoneme. This suggests that with some of the popular tests of auditory discrimination, factors other than auditory discrimination ability are being measured and exaggerated estimates of auditory discrimination difficulty are being made. (Hardy, 1973, p. 50)

The high error scores of backward readers compared to good readers have been studied by Blank who has drawn attention to the tendency for the excess of errors to be on the pairs differing in the final phoneme. She has stated that:

> A variety of complex processes are involved in what appears to be simple perceptual discrimination. For example, the two words must be attended to, retained and internally and sequentially compared and a judgment of their similarity must be made. (Blank, 1968, p. 1092)

The association between results on the Wepman Test of Auditory Discrimination and verbal tests when young children are studied has been reported by Deutsch (1967); while the significance of social class variables to both high error scores on the Wepman and to poor reading are discussed by Blank in *Language and Poverty* (Blank 1970). These findings would thus lend support to the views expressed in this chapter that the success of the fluent readers on this task of discrimination of like-sounding words should be viewed in a context of language development, rather than as an indication of better developed auditory discrimination *per se* than the children with whom their results have been compared. It can no more be said that good auditory discrimination is the cause of their success in learning to read than that their auditory discrimination can be explained away as resulting from their reading skill. It is yet further evidence of the awareness of these children who are fluent readers of the discriminations which are of significance in the language context in which they are rapidly developing such fluency.

CHAPTER V

Early Experiences and Home Background

Although the first testing of attainment and intelligence was completed in the school attended by the fluent readers, the mothers were
invited subsequently to bring their children to the university. While
the child was being further assessed, the parent accompanying the
child was interviewed on topics related to the family background,
the child's early development and the parent's perception of the
factors which had contributed to the early reading of that particular
child in the family. All parents responded favourably to the approach;
one parent, although unwilling to come to the university, agreed to
be interviewed in the child's school. Most children were brought by
their mother; both parents accompanied several children and were
interviewed together; while in three instances the father alone was
interviewed. A second interview was held several years later to discuss the children's further progress; all of these second interviews
took place in 1973. Several parents and some teachers contacted the
author in the intervening period for advice or assistance. All but
three families attended on the second occasion although no pressure
was placed on parents to attend the second interview and no remin-
ders were sent. The three missing children were a boy and a girl
who had left the district and the girl whose parent had initially been
interviewed in the school. On the second occasion also, several
children were accompanied by both parents though this had
necessitated the father at least obtaining time off work. Few parents
were willing to accept travelling expenses offered on any occasion
they visited the university although some travelled a considerable
distance, saying that they felt it was for the good of their child and
that they would therefore be embarrassed to accept payment.

It was hoped to obtain from the interviews certain basic information about home background and the features of early experiences
which had been shown in other studies to be either characteristic of
early readers – or regarded as significant in the development of
children who were later shown to have severe reading difficulties.
Thus, not only the positive aspects of the home experiences were
explored, but also the birth history, early illnesses, separation and

other similar aspects. In the absence of a control group it is, of course, not possible to make direct comparisons of significance of the kind which are to be found in Durkin's study (Durkin 1966). Such explorations of the negative as well as the positive characteristics none the less proved to be a valuable aspect of the information obtained from the interviews. A further 'bonus' from this aspect of the study was the fascinating and significant insights into the language interaction between these children and their parents gained from observations during their visit to the university. Time spent chatting to the parents and children in the waiting-room, or observing the exchanges of experiences between child and adult when they were reunited – or even the interaction between the adult and any younger siblings who accompanied them was more than amply repaid. Though not quantifiable, such contacts on both visits profoundly affected the author's thoughts on parent-child interaction and its significance for language development. One boy, as reported by his parents on the second visit, had asked whether they thought the waiting-room was 'bugged'! Had it been, the information obtained would indeed have been valuable! The parents were, however, informed of any occasion on which a recording was being made and the waiting-room was free from such intrusion.

While basic guidelines were prepared in advance for the parental interviews, it was found necessary, because of the wide range of backgrounds from which the children came, to allow a certain variation in approach in eliciting information. When the earlier interviews were being coded it was found that answers to certain questions later found to be important had not been obtained from all the parents; in such instances these were obtained in writing from the remaining parents. All parents were also asked to complete the Rutter questionnaire (Child Scale A) at the time of the initial interview (Rutter, Tizard and Whitmore 1970). This, it was hoped, would give information which could be compared with that obtained from two of the child's teachers who completed Child Scale B, some of whose questions are similar to those on the parental questionnaire.

Home and Family Background

With regard to size of family, place in family, parent's occupation and other such characteristics, these thirty-two children showed as wide a diversity as in other aspects discussed so far. As may be seen in Table 11, though some of the fluent readers were 'only' children at the time they started school, or were from small families, larger families were also represented. Place in family also varied; some

Table 11. Position in Family of Fluent Readers at Beginning of Study

Size of Family	Frequency	Place in Family	
I	3*	Only	
2	17*	10 elder	7 younger
3	7	2 second	4 younger
4	2	2 youngest	
5	2	1 fourth	1 younger
6, 7	0	—	
8	1	1 sixth	
Total	32		

* Two children were adopted.

were elder children but a number were younger or youngest. While some of those who had older brothers or sisters had been read to by their siblings, or had listened to their siblings practising reading at home, in at least one instance, the parents reported having to take steps to avoid the younger precocious reader embarrassing his older sibling who was learning to read at the normal time and in the usual way with the assistance of a reading scheme, unnecessary to the younger child. While there was a varied pattern with regard to size of family and place in family the age of the mother on the birth of the fluent reader was higher than normal. None of the mothers was known to be under twenty at the time of the birth (the possible exceptions were the two adopted children) and fifteen were known to be over thirty years of age. (See Table 12.) The warmth of

Table 12. Age of Mother on Birth of Child in Present Study

	Age of Mother				
	20+	25+	30+	35+	40+
Frequency	5	7	8	3	4
Adopted			2		
Not Known			3		
Total			32		

interest shown by these mothers in their children's development was outstanding and this may be related among other things to their age at the time of the birth. This child in one instance was the first live birth after a succession of miscarriages, and when the mother was asked what her expectations for the child had been (the child in question being outstandingly intelligent) she replied that she was only relieved he had lived and was normal. While modest in any claims they made for their contribution to the precocious reading performance of their children, the mothers all expressed interest in their child's progress and found the children stimulating companions. Few had worked, even part-time, while the children were of pre-school age – or had sent their children either to a nursery school or play group. One explanation for the finding that only six had attended nursery school (five girls and one boy) could have been the limited provision of such facilities at the time these children were young; the significant feature was the responses made by the mothers and their consistency over the two interviews. The second interview was in 1973 after the announcement of the government's commitment to nursery education for all children whose parents wish it (*Framework for Expansion* D.E.S. 1972). Each parent was asked not only whether her child had attended a nursery school but also if she knew what provision was available in her area; on the second occasion she was asked whether she would send her child to nursery school were one readily available.

The lack of desire to send their children to nursery schools shown by a number of the parents was not linked with a lack of respect for the value of education. Far from it, even these parents who had themselves left school at an early age showed concern that their families should not do likewise. Nursery-school education was not yet seen by these parents as playing a role that was related to later education; where it was mentioned as valuable it was by those parents whose children had no readily available companions of a similar age or siblings with whom to play. Several parents remarked that had their child been less willing to concentrate and more troublesome, or yearned for further company, then they might have thought differently. Although few of the children were described as not being liked by other children, a number were described by their parents, when completing the questionnaire, as tending 'to do things on their own – rather solitary'. This was also one of the items singled out for a number of children by both teachers who completed the questionnaire. Certainly many of these children seemed well able to absorb themselves in activities with a high level of concentration and although they welcomed children's company on occasion, they were self-sufficient enough to occupy themselves in its absence.

These mothers were fortunate from one point of view in being able to carry out household duties without incessant interruptions; it was also quite clear that they welcomed rather than rebuffed attempts at verbal interaction by the children and that they provided them with a variety of interesting materials with which to occupy themselves.

The fact that these children were already reading fluently meant that they had a further activity available to them at this early age. It should, however, be borne in mind that as they were learning to read, or indeed as they tackled absorbing but progressively more difficult books, they were still likely to require instant assistance from an adult to supply them with any word which could not be understood from the context. These adults seemed willing to provide such instant encouragement and also to take part in play with their children even at the expense of delaying their other activities.

It was certainly clear that these parents did not feel a need to obtain outside assistance with their children's education at the pre-school stage though several of the children did attend a pre-school play group at least briefly. Such attendance is, however, limited to a few sessions weekly and the active involvement of the mother is also required. This lack of a desire by the parents for frequent regular outside provision for the children at the pre-school stage was probably related to the mothers' lack of desire to obtain work outside the home or to resume their career; it was certainly not a simple cause and effect relationship but rather one feature of their respect for the needs of, and enjoyment in, the company of their young families. While few of the mothers were working, even part time, when the children first started school, a surprising number were still, on the occasion of the second interview, either not working or only part-time and in such a way that they were home for lunch or to greet their children on their return from school.

A contentment and satisfaction with the role of mother and a deep involvement with their children's interests was clearly evident and made it a pleasure to interview these parents on both occasions. Few of the parents were in any way boastful of their children's superiority; they were on the contrary rather self-conscious and embarrassed. The enthusiasm was evident from the graphic way they could relive experiences they had shared with the children – or even capture the spirit of the original in reporting an incident which they had not shared initially first hand with the child. One example of this was the vivid way one mother described her child's first testing for the present study, capturing the spirit of the child's original interview although she had only shared this at second-hand. The absorption of these parents in their home life and their shared family experiences is all the more interesting when one considers that some of the mothers had previously followed careers which they still in 1973 showed no sign of resuming. Where both parents were interviewed this same enthusiasm for home life as an exciting experience was equally clear. Adequacy of finance was not it seemed a deciding factor in determining whether or not the mother should work, since in some instances the fathers worked a great deal of overtime to assist with the family budget.

Parental Education and Occupational Status

Social class is frequently quoted as an important variable in defining the status of the home and the likely attitude to education. Recently, however, the importance of considering the length of schooling of the parents and particularly the mother's further education or training has been appreciated. The ages on leaving school of both parents may be seen in Table 13. In the case of the two adopted children

Table 13. Age on Leaving School of Parents of Fluent Readers

| | Age on Leaving School | | | | | | |
	14+	15+	16+	17+	18+	Not Known	Total
Father	5	12	2	6	5	2	32
Mother	5	9	1	9	7	1	32

these refer to the adoptive parents. Few of the mothers had married early and most had some employment and often additional training before marriage. The details of further education and training of both parents are shown in Table 14. A number of fathers were in the professions; some were, however, in unskilled employment or unemployed.

As mentioned earlier, even those parents who had left school early seemed determined to ensure that *their* children, not just the fluent reader, should avoid making the same mistake. One mother had left school at an early age, as had her husband; he had an unskilled job with long hours, while she also had an unskilled part-time job. Both, however, were avid readers and she described how on occasion they would sit absorbed in books and this seemed a shared social experience rather than the isolated activity it is sometimes considered. To quote, 'We could be sitting quiet for hours just reading.' In another family, the mother who was one of a large family, had left school at an early age, as had the father, who was so bored that he had truanted frequently. Neither parent had followed any formal course of study after leaving school. The fluent reader in this family was the youngest of four children. For all, books formed a fascinating part of their life and a shared experience. On occasion the father would read to the children; he confessed he loved fairy stories himself. All six

Table 14. Details of Further Education and Training of Parents

Description	Totals	Comments
Both parents left school at 14/15 no certificate from school or further training	6	—
One parent left school with certificate – other no further training	3	(2 fathers 1 mother with certificate)
Both parents certif. from school but no further training	1	(left school at 15)
One parent had further training – other no certif. or training	6	(4 fathers, 2 mothers had further training)
One parent further training – other certif. from school	1	(1 father further training)
Both parents professional or further training after leaving school	3	—
One parent prof. training or certif. from school – other parent attended university	7	(3 fathers with degrees and 2 mothers, also 2 mothers attended university but did not complete)
Both parents have degree	3	—
Incomplete information	2	(Known not to have degree or professional training)
Total number of families	32	

Information for adopted children refers to adoptive parents.

used the local library regularly and even on occasion read books selected by one of the others. Thus, here also, written and spoken language were experienced in a warm and accepting social context. The richness of support for education which these and several other families in the study were providing was not measurable on scales such as social class, father's occupation, mother's education – or even number of books in the house. Although in the homes of the two children referred to above as in those of several others in the study, there was a limited supply of purchased books, there was extensive use of library facilities. The lesson from these interviews was a clear one that it is crucial to explore the parents' perceptions of education and the support and experiences they provide by measures far more sensitive and penetrating than social class, father's occupation – or even education of the parents. These homes were providing rich and exciting experiences within which books were indeed an integral part. Clearly the selection of these particular children who were

already fluent readers on beginning school had led to the investigation of some families whose contribution to the education of their
children is little recognized and less respected.

In only one of these families was a sibling also reading fluently on
starting school and that was a professional family of very gifted
children. It should be stated, however, that although the children in
this study read prior to school age, with all the disadvantages as
well as advantages that presented, most of the siblings from these
same families were successful in school, even those from homes where
the parents had themselves left school early. For this reason some of
the features of these successful homes seem to be of vital importance
to a fuller and clearer understanding of the factors contributing to
success in school. The role of parents in early and in later education
is too often seen as one of acceptance of the offerings of the formal
educational system or of 'preparing' the child for school. The contribution of these parents to the success in education of their families
could never be measured by the usual yardsticks. Clearly it is
unrealistic to expect the kind and quality of information elicited in
the interviews in this study to be obtained for all children in school
at a variety of stages. It is, however, unjustified to attribute the
success of such children to the school merely because the cruder
measures of social class, parents' education and so on, led one to
anticipate failure or mediocrity. Just as it is important to consider
the attributes of the child who succeeds when our 'at risk' estimates
would have led to a prediction of failure, it is equally important to
consider the qualities in the homes where the majority of the children
are more successful than would have been predicted. It seems
important to consider further the background and the characteristics
of the fluent readers themselves as seen by their parents in order
to determine the extent to which, and, the ways in which, they
or their pre-school experiences were different from the rest of the
family.

Birth History and Early Development

For thirteen of the fluent readers, the birth was described as difficult;
the remaining eighteen were said to be normal births (there was no
information for one child). Reasons for describing the births as difficult included forceps delivery breech birth, caesarian section, in-
duced birth and one for whom oxygen was required because the cord
was round his neck. In addition three of the mothers who described
the births as normal suffered from high blood pressure or toxaemia
during pregnancy. In view of the age distribution of the mothers on

the birth of this particular child there would of course be a greater than average risk of a difficult birth, prolonged labour or other complications. It is important to note, in the light of the tendency to assume a causal connection in a child who later develops language or reading difficulties, that one third of the children in this study were reported as having had difficult births.

While several of the children had a succession of illnesses in their early years, two suffering from bronchial asthma, another from kidney trouble, and several had accidents resulting in concussion, it would be quite misleading to suggest that they were a group of unhealthy or isolated children. Several had, at various times pre-school, been separated from their mothers because of either their own ill-health or that of their mothers. It was clear that arrangements had been made to ensure that they were looked after and if possible prepared for such situations. When asked about walking, talking, toilet training etc., the parents did not tend to regard these children as in advance of their siblings. A number of parents did, however, mention this child as particularly sensitive, as easily anxious or as crying easily, in comparison to the other children in the family. 'Restlessness' was mentioned by a number of parents. In the light of further questioning it appeared that this was the normal outgoing activity for pre-school children rather than an abnormal restlessness. It should, further, be borne in mind that the majority of the group were boys. In short, the mothers did not regard the early physical development of these children as either abnormally slow or strikingly in advance of the rest of the family.

The only reported incidence of difficulties in close relations were three retarded children and the sister of one parent and the brother of another who had attended reading clinics.

Left-handedness or slow development of dominant handedness is still frequently quoted as a significant feature in children who later develop reading or language difficulties, in spite of a failure of large-scale surveys to substantiate this association. (See Clark 1970 for a reference to a number of such studies.) In this group three of the twenty boys were using their left hand for writing at the time of starting school and two boys and one girl used either hand. The three left-handed boys had Stanford Binet IQs of 139, 140 and 165, and reading ages on the Schonell Graded Reading Test of ten years eleven months, nine years four months and eleven years five months on starting school. The three children of mixed handedness had S.B. IQs of 143, 148 and 149 and reading ages of eleven years ten months, eight years eight months and nine years ten months. It is worth noting that one of the boys of mixed handedness had a reading level of over eleven years of age for accuracy, and the ability to read the daily paper with understanding on starting school. His spelling was also on the level of a ten-year-old. His mother reported high blood pressure during pregnancy and an earlier history of frequent miscarriages, while the child suffered from concussion at an early age. Had he shown reading difficulties, these factors might well have been seen to be causally connected. This child's mixed handedness he used to good effect when drawing the Mazes in the WPPSI, using whichever hand made it easier to see what he was doing as he completed the task! While it must be agreed that he showed skill, rather than lack of skill with both hands, it is, none the less, important to draw attention to these cases which on some 'at risk' registers would score a number of points. One of the other boys who was left-handed and an avid reader of advanced books from an early age achieved this though his motor-co-ordination was poor. His mother indeed commented at the second interview that his teacher had remarked with amusement on his difficulties when tying shoe laces at a time when he could read and converse intelligently on a variety of subjects. This mother who was herself right-handed commented that the attempts by herself and her husband to assist their son in tying his laces had probably added to his confusion. It is worth noting further that of the six children referred to above, all were spelling at least on the level of a seven-year-old, and the three of mixed handedness were spelling at over a nine-year-old level when first tested. Although it would of course be dangerous to generalize from evidence from six intelligent children, it is, however, worth noting that they learned both to read and to spell without effort, without change of handedness *and* at an early age. *In preparing criteria of children at risk it is imperative that our very instruments do not lead to an expectation of failure by some children on the part of their parents or teachers.* Most of the children discussed here seemed to develop their early skills in oral language, in reading and in writing in a warm accepting and non-pressurized environment where the parents were guided by their child's interests and where indeed some parents even felt embarrassed at their children's rapid and excessively early progress towards literacy. At this early pre-school stage they were not anticipating failure but rather marvelling at the rapid and apparently effortless success of their children. It was difficult in the interviews to separate the book experiences from the rest of the pre-school background of these children. An attempt will be made to identify what appeared to be the crucial features in these children's development which led to their early literacy.

Early Reading and Related Experiences

One factor which emerged clearly during the interviews was the bewilderment and even embarrassment on the part of some of the parents at having a child who started school already reading fluently – a task which they saw as the prerogative of the school. Several described attempts to discourage the child at first until, as one mother described it, she realized it was impossible, and that the child gave every appearance of being sufficiently fluent by the time she started school so that being able to read would not present a problem. Another mother described the adverse comments of neighbours who assumed she must have coached the child at the expense of other aspects of development. Only a few parents had made a conscious and systematic attempt to teach their child to read with the aid of graded readers of the kind used in school reading instruction or of flash cards. Even then it was clear that several were taking this step as a result of, not in order to develop, interests expressed by the child.

A list of the questions which formed the basis for the exploration of early reading experiences is to be found in Appendix A. In addition to answering the precise question, most parents added interesting extensive or explanatory comments. Within this section an attempt will be made to give as faithful a portrayal of these interviews as possible without resort to frequent tables.

Half of the parents felt their child's present reading level had been established for between one and two years, the remainder being divided equally between less than a year and more than two years. The children read a variety of print – non-fiction was mentioned almost as often as fiction and comics and the daily papers were also each mentioned by over one third of the parents. Indeed the parents of one child commented that it was odd to have a father unable to read his daily paper because his five-year-old son was there first. Sports news and television programmes were two of the sources of interest in the newspapers to the boys in particular. The girls tended to be interested in reading for themselves stories they had already heard, or stories of a similar level. The boys on the contrary, even at the time of the initial interview, were inclined to show interest in the print in their environment and to use their reading skill to extend their knowledge – often in ways and at levels which the adults would not have considered appropriate at such an early age. Two of the children were already reading adult books. Several of the parents found the question about type of reading difficult to answer as they felt their child 'devoured' anything in print that was available. While some of the children inherited their books from siblings, or received them as presents, more than half of the children were already making use of the public library. Twenty of the children had their own ticket and many went at least once a week. One mother laughingly described faking her child's age so that he could have his own ticket before the age of five! One child was allowed to go on her own to join the nearby public library on the suggestion of her teacher; another showed the initiative of obtaining a form for himself from the library and bringing it for his parents to sign. These children already seemed to be developing tastes and preferences in books; to be self-sufficient enough to find books of their choice in the library and to choose their own books at other times also. Where the parents themselves used the library or where there was an interested and helpful children's librarian these children were able to obtain stimulating reading material. Occasionally this was not so successful. One mother of a very bright child, finding difficulty in securing suitable reading material for him, asked in the library for a particular book she had enjoyed as a child but when that was not available was rather at a loss. Unfortunately in that library there was not a readily available adult to give advice. The local library was a crucial source of reading material for these children even at this early stage, but particularly when they were re-interviewed several years later. Few obtained sufficiently exciting or stimulating reading material through the school or in great enough quantities. It therefore seems particularly important that librarians be on the look-out for such children – especially those whose parents, though supportive, do not have the background knowledge to advise their children and to develop their tastes further. Several of the children had received some help from teachers or relatives but few had found the school class libraries helpful, even by the time of the second interview. It is important that neither the local libraries nor the school libraries should restrict children's choice of books merely on account of age. Variations in accessibility of reading materials whether fiction or non-fiction, was evident in the libraries. In some cases age was an absolute barrier to certain types of books, in others it was not. Some families managed to overcome this by borrowing books from the local library on the parents' tickets while in other families where the parents were not members themselves, books were either bought or borrowed. The restrictive policies were particularly limiting on some of the boys who wanted access to encyclopedias and other non-fiction books. About a third of the parents still read to the children when they started school (almost as many fathers as mothers) some reading from the same books as the children themselves read, others choosing different stories. Some parents found that the children no longer wished to be read to when they themselves could read. Many of the children when asked who read to them mentioned both mother and father. One girl replied, 'Mummy used to, I read to Mummy now.'

When the children were reading for themselves, if they could not guess a strange word, they were reported as either asking someone or attempting to sound it out. The children themselves were also asked what they did if when reading they got stuck and didn't know a word. A number replied that they would ask their mother or father. They were also asked what they would do if they were busy or not available. The replies included: 'I just go on to the next word and see if I know what it was' – 'spell it out' – 'sound it first' 'just keep trying or tell my mother and she'll tell me. If she's not there I just miss it out' and finally 'take it syllable by syllable that's what my Dad told me' (age four years eleven months). While a number of the children were first attracted to reading through stories, a number began with signs, advertisements, or letter games. Although these early reading experiences for some of the children were in books from which they had enjoyed stories, for some of the children the print in their immediate environment played an important role. This was particulary true of the boys who showed interest in sign-posts, car names, captions on television and names on products at the supermarkets. We tend to under-estimate the extent to which television supplies, in the commercials, frequent visual and auditory learning material, simultaneously presented in a form which a well-motivated child could utilize for learning a basic sight vocabulary. This learning is later reinforced when identifying the products on the shelves of the supermarket or in the cupboard. It did not seem, however, that the parents artificially arranged a learning situation in which their child was led specifically to appreciate the charac-teristics of print, but rather that the print was one of the characteris-tics which distinguished the products and was therefore attended to by child and parents. The parents found it very difficult to describe precisely how the children acquired the basic skill of reading – several mentioned that the child copied a sibling or learned a story by heart. A few mothers taught the sounds of the letters or the names of the letters to the children; more acquired the names of letters before the sounds, the sounds being associated with writing rather than reading, in which most of the children were also interested.

Already before four years of age, ten of the children were also interested in writing. Some began by copying words, others letters, a few wrote their names or little messages – while one wrote the football scores. Over half the children used blackboards but most also used pencil and paper. Few of the parents had guided the children's hands but had merely given encouragement. Many of the blackboards had letters printed on them – often in capitals which is possibly why so many favoured capitals rather than lower case letters in writing when they were tested in spelling in this study.

Children's Knowledge of Terms Used in Reading

Following on the work of Reid (1966), Downing (1969) and Hardy (1973) on children's knowledge of the terms used in early reading instruction it was decided to explore these children's knowledge on starting school of terms such as 'word', 'letter', and 'sentence' and whether they could explain or give examples of the difference between the names and sounds of the letters. Most of the children could give an example of a word and a letter which showed they understood the difference; a number could also give an example of a sentence. Some also attempted to explain the characteristics of a *word* as:

> 'I'm using words right now – they are made up of letters, they are things you speak.'
> 'Something you say when talking to somebody.'
> 'A thing you read in a book.' 'Something you spell.'
> 'It's got a lot of letters in it and it spells something.'

a *letter* as:

> 'A part of a word or a postman brings it.'
> 'Some pieces of line that make a letter.'
> 'Bit of a word – something that builds up words.'
> 'Anything in the alphabet.'

a *sentence* as:

> 'If you are caught you are sentenced – a thing you answer.'
> 'It's like a question.' (gave an example)
> 'It's a lot of words and then a dot at the end.'
> 'Some words put together – if it is not a sentence it's just a jumble of words.'

A few of the children could explain the difference between 'the name' and 'the sound' of a letter – as one child answered, 'you mean calling "S" sss'. Only a minority of the children could explain the difference between letters and words but most could give or even gave spontaneously examples which showed their awareness. None

gave as an example a number in error for a letter. Most of the
children when giving an example of a letter gave the name and not
the sound, confirming the comment from the parents that they
tended to use the names of the letters to their children.

Explanations for the above concepts were given by only a few of
the group; some examples are, however, quoted above to show the
range of which they were capable at about five years of age. These
tended, as would be expected, to be given by the more intelligent
children as may be seen from the double meaning of 'sentence' and
'letter' volunteered by one boy and also by those whose parents
would easily and lucidly have given explanations themselves. Most
of the children could indicate their awareness of the distinction
between the concepts although unable to verbalize this. Attention is
being directed by a number of research workers, including Reid,
Downing and Hardy, to the need to ensure that children understand
the concepts in early reading instruction; this should not be taken
to mean that the children in order to learn to read need to be able to
give adequate verbal explanations for these.

Help with Reading

The parents were asked who had helped the child most with reading
or been most involved. This help for the majority was before four
years of age and the mother was mentioned twice as often as the
father, while siblings were occasionally mentioned or another relative.
In few cases were those helping experienced in teaching reading. While
half the parents felt the children were helped daily many stressed
that this help was at odd times as requested, that it was casual rather
than systematic, and that it was part of their daily life rather than
something separate.

Only six of the mothers had read any books about teaching children to read and several of these were teachers themselves. Five of
the parents said they had encouraged the child to make a start in
learning to read but twenty-five insisted that the initial interest was
from the child and that they gradually or even as mentioned earlier,
reluctantly responded to requests for help! A few of the parents had
themselves been reported as reading before they started school and
it was of course not possible to determine how fluent they had been
at the same stage. Some of the siblings were also beginning to read
before starting school but not on the level of the present child.

The parents were asked to consider ways in which the child in this
study differed from the other children in the family. This they found
difficult to answer with regard to aspects not specifically concerned

with their early reading. Some mentioned that these children were less outgoing or had better concentration than others. It is, however, hard to separate cause and effect. Indeed one mother commented that the others in the family read quickly after starting school. Clearly the young fluent readers had some personal characteristics which did differentiate them from their siblings. It is difficult to generalize them across the study and even to separate them from characteristics which were the result of their fluency in reading print with understanding. Their memory for precise detail with regard to events was commented on by several parents; here again one parent at least noted that a sibling who was not an early fluent reader had an even better memory for certain types of event. Attempts to assess the precise characteristics of these children are perhaps more appropriately based on their results on standardized tests discussed in earlier chapters. It is worth noting here that several parents commented that circumstances resulted in this particular child having access to an adult with time to spare and an interest in reading to them and answering questions for them which their siblings had not. For example some of the children had much older brothers or sisters who took a particular interest; another had an aunt, another a grandmother who happened to be available to that child pre-school, yet another father was off work for an extended period. It would oversimplify the relationships and interaction involved and indeed the qualities in the child necessary for such precocious reading development to suggest this is the only feature which differentiates this group of children. Nevertheless it is important to note the presence of an interested adult with time to spare to interact in a stimulating encouraging environment and to consider the extent to which this is one pre-requisite for learning to read in a language context.

Play Activities

While nine of the children were said to prefer to spend time with adults, a number did prefer to play with children when these were available. Few played with younger children but usually of their own age or older. They were described as playing normal childish games, imaginative games, jigsaw puzzles and other construction games were mentioned by several. When other children were not available they seemed generally to be very self-sufficient. When not reading they would draw or play with cars or dolls, or lego – or three mentioned that they would talk with mother.

All but two of the children watched television and only five of the parents felt that the child had learned nothing from watching. Only one parent, however, said the child watched unselectively. Indeed in many instances the children were themselves selecting after consulting the day's viewing details. Several programmes connected with reading were mentioned and also other information programmes and the schools broadcasts. Television viewing was again discussed at the later interview and then also the children were themselves described as selective, either leaving the room if not interested, or absorbing themselves in a book to the exclusion of all else. Encouragement in the development of selectivity *by the child* was a striking feature in many aspects of the lives of these families. Children were assisted to make choices rather than have choices made for them.

Starting School

The parents were questioned on the school's reactions to their child's fluent reading. Few of the parents informed the school initially; their embarrassment at their children's early fluency making them reticent. Indeed several children sat quietly for several months without revealing their skill. Three parents commented on the fact that the school their child attended used 'ita' and that they were concerned that this might cause difficulties (five of the children attended 'ita' schools). One parent on the advice of a friend who was a teacher, informed the infant teacher that her child could read, feeling this was necessary because he was attending an 'ita' school. The infant teacher later reported that she was prepared to take this with 'a pinch of salt' but passed a letter to the child which was meant for his mother. Not only did he read it correctly, but he also reacted with a sigh and a comment at the prospect of the next seven years in the school in question! While some of the teachers were described as pleased to learn the child could read and as having said this would give the child scope, others were described as indifferent or claiming that this would reduce the child's scope. Half of the children were described as extremely interested in school, most of the rest were, at that stage, at least adequately interested.

The embarrassment of these parents and their diffidence at reporting their child's abilities, and the rebuff which some met when they did, seem matters of concern. With the expansion of nursery education and the encouragement of more parents to become involved in story reading to their children it may be anticipated that more children will come to school already reading with understanding. This will not necessarily reflect a conscious or premature policy of instruction but the increased access to children's books of some children for whom these would not previously have been available, together with increased adult-child interaction, which is being advocated both in the homes and in the pre-school establishments. Far from being a more homogeneous group of 'ready' pupils starting school, readiness may be very differently distributed. With this it will be necessary to consider the extent to which the nursery schools will be 'blamed' as some of these parents felt reproached for the too early introduction of instruction in reading when the skill has in effect developed as a natural outcome of the situation in which the child has found himself – coupled, of course, with particular characteristics and motivation in the individual child. Nursery teachers are already asking themselves whether they should teach reading or even whether they should discourage the child who seems absorbed with books to the exclusion of other activities. Some primary teachers seem uninterested in obtaining information on a child's previous relevant experiences whether they be within the nursery school or the home. Education does not begin at five years of age, or indeed on entry to school. While there is a great deal of discussion on children who come to school 'unready', there is perhaps not enough interest in, or even awareness of, the skills that the child brings to the school situation whether he be reading or not. Children starting school never were, and never will be, any more homogeneous in their awareness of the characteristics of print than they are with regard to understanding and expressive oral language development. Where the school situation is so structured that only certain responses are permitted and encouraged then the skills may appear superficially to be within a narrow range. Though one should not minimize the problems that these early fluent readers present in the classroom, it is important to stress that they are indeed the end of a continuum and may therefore highlight problems faced by many children on starting school.

In the following chapter the information obtained from the schools over the period of the research will be discussed, before turning to a consideration of the children's interests two years later and their parents' perception of their early development seen in retrospect.

CHAPTER VI

The First Few Years at School

The results of the attainment tests administered to the fluent readers shortly after beginning school were discussed in Chapter II and information from the parents about the children's early development and initial adjustment to school has been reported in the preceding chapter. Additional information on adjustment to school was obtained from the teachers at the beginning of the research when the children were starting school and again at the end of 1972. The head teachers and class teachers were asked also at the end of 1972 to complete forms giving information about attainment in relation to others in the class, interest in books, concentration, acceptability to other children and other factors thought to be relevant. (See Appendix B.) The information on adjustment was obtained from different teachers on the two occasions; the second teacher from whom information was obtained both on adjustment and attainment being likely to have only limited knowledge of the child's early referral to the study and certainly not to have had any responsibility for singling the child out for referral. A number of head teachers had changed since the beginning of the study and five children had changed school while still remaining in the study, thus the later information was not from a person who had been deeply involved with the child initially.

Adjustment to School

The Rutter Scale B used in this study was similar to that used in the Isle of Wight Survey (Rutter, Tizard and Whitmore 1970) and was also used in the present author's study of children with reading difficulties (Clark 1970). It consists of twenty-six items which the teacher checks as 'doesn't apply', 'applies somewhat', 'certainly applies'. The items are descriptions of behaviour such as 'squirmy', 'fidgety child', 'is often disobedient', 'has poor concentration or short attention span'. Some items are of acting out behaviour, others of withdrawn behaviour. Two points are scored for items which certainly apply and one point for 'applies somewhat'. Thus the higher the score, the greater the number of negative attributes. Only five boys and one girl received any two point scores on the first occasion and only three on the second occasion. Ten children out of thirty-two and twelve out of the thirty remaining had no items marked even as applying somewhat by the first and second teachers respectively. Scores above nine, regarded as indicative of some disturbance, were obtained by only three children, one on the first occasion and two different children on the second. Two of these children had changed school – one prior to, and one after, the high score. Two had frequent absences and were distressed and tearful, one both in school and at home, the other at the prospect of changing to a new school. One child went through a period of severe distress, which fortunately was only temporary, but for which he was attending the doctor; and the form was completed during this period.

Where either teacher indicated behaviour on the scale as applying to any of these children the item tended to be of the type 'often worries, worries about many things', 'tends to do things on his own – rather solitary', 'tends to be fearful or afraid of new things or situations', or 'fussy or over-particular child', rather than the type mentioned above. No child received a high score from both teachers; the scores were generally even lower on the second than the first occasion. Items scored on either occasion were those indicative of sensitivity to new situations and even these tended to be noted as applying 'only somewhat'. It should be stressed that on the second occasion only two girls had any items marked and only four boys had a score of more than four. It would appear that some of the sensitivity noted on the first occasion may have been a reflection of the early stages of settling in to school. This would be in line with the information from the parents who both in the questionnaire and in interview tended to comment on the children's anxiety and sensitivity in new or strange situations. Thus, the fluent readers were still several years later perceived by their teachers as well-adjusted in school. This was confirmed by the responses given by the teachers to the following questions:

'Is he/she a leader in class YES/NO'
'Is he/she accepted by the children in the class YES/NO'

All were regarded as accepted by other children and eleven were also regarded as leaders. In response to the further question – 'Do you find he/she has good concentration or is easily distracted?' the teachers, almost without exception, replied describing the children as having excellent or good concentration. The following are some of the responses:

'When involved in a book is oblivious to anything else in the classroom' (at age 6+).
'Reads rapidly through the class library, very good powers of concentration' (at age 6+).
'tenacity of purpose and sustained effort', 'concentrates well on what he can do but welcomes distraction if in doubt!'
'Good concentration but gets bored with repetition.'
'Excellent concentration, remembers almost word for word what he has read or heard.'

Two children were described as restless and distractible, losing interest easily. One of these children was described in a similar manner by his mother. Although he was very advanced in reading, spelling and counting, it seemed difficult to sustain his interest. The other children in his family were not precocious nor particularly interested in books. The other child who was distractible had frequent absences and cried easily.

Clearly as a group these children were regarded not unfavourably by their teachers who considered them to have good concentration, wide interests and to be acceptable to other children. Many appear to have related well to their teachers as can be judged from some further examples of the comments made by their teachers:

'a delightful child'
'can see the ridiculous side of things before others'
'good background of knowledge, bright personality'
'has a thirst for knowledge'
'sense of humour and fun'

A tribute to one particular child is worth quoting in detail:

an asset and has many original ideas; witty in spoken and written word shows qualities of leadership and masterminds playground games much to the delight of his friends who seem flattered to be chosen for a trifling task. Obtains information to talk about rather than write about. Only when left to choose his own subject that his sparkle and high level of proficiency shows.

The final quotation above, speaks highly not only for that child, but for the teacher who reveals her own awareness of the needs of that child who had already in his short life suffered several tragedies and who could be timid and anxious under certain conditions. The richness of the verbal interchanges, the experiences and the fun of learning in that classroom are clearly evident from the teacher's graphic and sensitive answers to all the questions on the form.

Such an advanced level of reading as these children had on starting school could cause some problems for them in their early years at school. A number of teachers expressed their concern when these children first started school that they would find it difficult to stimulate them sufficiently. When their precocious reading was coupled, as it was in some instances, with a high level of intelligence and general knowledge well beyond their years, these children were a challenge to their teachers. By the time they had been several years at school, many were, however, being regarded by their teachers as 'an asset'. When the teachers used the description 'tends to do things on his own, rather solitary' as 'applying somewhat' it would seem therefore that they are regarding this as an independence, and *not* as indicating a rejection by other children. This would confirm the impression gained from a number of mothers that these children while enjoying the company of other children might sometimes reject company because they were already absorbed in some other activity. They were accepted by other children, could enjoy their company, but could also be contented when alone. The choice was theirs.

Promotion or Not?

It was quickly apparent to the school how advanced some of these children were in reading and related skills – and also that some of them were highly intelligent. It was felt that teachers, faced with the problem of occupying these children appropriately, would have considered whether or not to promote them to a higher class and by accelerating them avoid expecting them to progress through a reading scheme in the normal way. The head teacher and class teacher were therefore asked to record on the form whether the child was now in the same class as his age group and whether promotion had been considered. If the child had been promoted the teachers were asked whether this had resulted in any problems; if not they were asked the reasons for deciding against promotion.

Four of the girls were already in a selective school and none of these was promoted. Five of the remaining twenty-six children had been promoted to a class with slightly older children. There were few schools in which classes within an age group were arranged by ability. Acceleration or promotion to a higher class is unusual in Scottish schools and certainly much less common than retention for a further year in the first or second class of children who are either immature or have failed to make progress in learning to read.

A number of head teachers stated that promotion would not have been considered as it was felt that a child should progress through the seven classes in primary school; several stressed the socializing influences of the first few classes and would not have allowed a child to be promoted at that stage. Other comments referred more specifically to the child in question – that the child's achievement was confined to reading or that he or she was not advanced in number work; that motor co-ordination was poor or that the child was socially immature. Several teachers commented that promotion would have meant separating the child from his friends; while several reported that the mother had specifically requested that the child should not be promoted. One mother mentioned when interviewed in the course of the study that she had asked that her son be promoted but that the school had not agreed. She was now pleased that her request had been refused as her son, who had frequent absences, had been better able to make up work he missed.

Two of the five promoted children were in schools using 'ita' and this appeared to have been one of the factors influencing the decision. For one child the promotion was almost immediately on starting school. This child had just missed by a few days having been able to start school a year earlier and this promotion reunited him with friends with whom he had played prior to starting school. This promotion was a success, although the teacher commented that his art and hand work showed his immaturity. For another child who was promoted soon after starting school, it resulted in temporary distress as the child's immature behaviour was condoned and even encouraged by the other children. Another teacher also mentioned similar problems and reported that when she checked the child the other children defended him. She then had to point out that if he was in that class he must adhere to the standards of behaviour set for the class. One of the children showed distress after leaving his friends and took some time to settle in the other class.

All the promoted children were still described as accepted by the children in their class; none were, however, described as leaders. None obtained high scores on the Rutter Scale on the second occasion after promotion, which would have suggested maladjustment. One child described as distressed and unsettled had also been so prior to promotion.

All the promoted children were still regarded as high or very high in reading accuracy and comprehension in relation to their present class. Four were very high in spelling; the remaining child was low. In composition a different child was low, two others were average and the remaining two high. The child who was low in spelling and composition had been noted as not interested in written work when first seen. In arithmetic all but that same child were rated as high or very high. The children's immaturity was, however, evident in their writing where four were regarded as low in ability and most were also low in art and handwork. They were average in games and physical education so their gross body movements must have been adequate. None was regarded as above average in music.

Thus in reading accuracy and comprehension, in spelling and in arithmetic these children could hold their own with older children. Several had problems with handwriting which was both slow and badly formed. Examples of their written work was sent and it was clear that several would have problems in showing their knowledge and creative abilities in written work as a result of their handwriting problems. Since most of the children in this study had a tendency to be sensitive and easily distressed, problems might arise for those whose motor-co-ordination was insufficient for written work of the standard required.

The children who were promoted were not necesssarily either the most intelligent, advanced or mature children in the study. The decision to promote was taken as a result of circumstances at a particular point in their school career. Some might not have been promoted in a different school – and several schools had at least temporary doubts as to whether they had made the correct decision – or at least whether they would make the same decision on a subsequent occasion. Faced with a child who is clearly well advanced and who appears bored or not sufficiently stimulated in his present class it is a difficult decision to face. It is also one which in some instances cannot successfully be reversed once made. Children do become careless or may make errors not only because work is too difficult, but also because it is too easy – or too repetitive. Further, where a child is bored, restless and unsettled yet well advanced in his school work, acceleration to a more taxing environment may indeed prove the answer; but not always.

In considering whether to promote a child it would seem important to consider the following aspects of the child's development.

1. Is the ability evident in a wide range of the basic subjects?
2. Has the child sufficient motor co-ordination to meet the demands of written work in the other class?
3. Is the child socially mature enough to cope with the change and is he sufficiently secure to fit into the new environment?
4. Has he close friends in his present class whom he would miss and is there evidence that he has any friends among the older children with whom he would have to mix?
5. Is his attendance regular enough to avoid problems in keeping pace with the more advanced work and, finally –
6. Would the parents be happy were their child to be promoted or

would they feel from their knowledge of the child, that the strange and demanding situation might be distressing?

Many children showing symptoms at home of severe strain as a result of school may in school appear superficially to be coping adequately. For this reason, apart from their right to be involved in such a decision, the views of the parents are critical in obtaining a full picture of the situation. A further aspect to be considered in which the parents' views are important is what the effect of promotion would be not only on that child, in isolation, but also in the family context, especially on relationships with siblings – particularly whether there is an older, less precocious sibling in the higher class. If the school is large enough to have more than one parallel class the situation would be very different from that where the two children would be in the same class – especially if there was already any stress at home as a result of the younger child's advanced level. One child was promoted into the same stage as a brother but the head teacher took care not to put them in the same class; in a smaller school this would not have been possible. In one family with two boys the younger boy was so 'advanced' that the mother had to stop the younger child, not yet at school, upsetting the older one learning to read. To place these two children in the same class would possibly have been disastrous for the older child – and have caused stress at home which might or might not have been detected by the busy teacher. One further point to be considered is the general policy of promotion in the area as well as the school. It seems pointless to promote a child if a few years later he will, on account of age, merely be expected to mark time in a class whose work he has already covered. This could be very unfortunate in leading the child to become careless in his work as a result of boredom, and also possibly a problem in the classroom.

In short, promotion or acceleration is no easy solution to provision of the stimulation and appropriate level of instruction either to the child with precocious reading ability or even of a high level of intellectual ability. The other factors listed above with regard to the child and the structure within the school need to be considered. As a short term policy promotion might alleviate immediate problems – or cause them. While not suggesting that such a decision should never be made it is important to stress the need to appreciate the complexity of the situation and the need to consider the longer term ramifications.

Since the evidence from the teachers and parents revealed these children to have a tendency to be sensitive, easily distressed and as setting very high standards for themselves, it seems particularly important to consider any question of promotion or indeed any form of special treatment from the point of view of its effect on that particular child, his strengths and his weaknesses, taking account of his personality as well as his attainment.

Attainment in School

The work of the children who were promoted was discussed separately because they were being compared by their teachers with children older than themselves. The remaining twenty-five children were in the class for their age group. Their pattern of attainment was rather similar to that reported for the five promoted children. All were regarded as high or very high in reading attainment and all but one also in reading comprehension. All but three were also high or very high in spelling and in composition; all but five were high or very high in arithmetic. In all the above subjects the rest of the children were average rather than low. In handwriting nine were rated as only average and two as low, while most were only average in art, handwork, physical education and games, three were high in music.

In short, as a group these children had a high level of attainment in relation to their group as perceived by their teachers. This was true for reading, spelling and composition. Many of them were also found by their teachers to be intelligent and stimulating in their oral language.

The teachers were asked what kind of books the children enjoyed and whether they had any problems in keeping them supplied with reading material. Few teachers mentioned any difficulty. It should, however, be noted that most of the children were not only members of the local library but used it extensively and a number were already borrowing from the adult section or were reading books which their parents had borrowed for themselves. The teachers mentioned interest in non-fiction books including science, geography and space books particularly among the boys as well as a range of fiction. One of the boys, who was not promoted and who was described as a charming boy but shy and retiring with his own age group in class, had been allowed to join the chess club normally open only to senior boys. He could already play chess before joining the club, was reported as mixing well with the boys in the chess club and as reading widely on chess also. This was evidence of one way of providing additional stimulation for this boy who was felt to be better placed with his own age group during school hours. It seems a pity that such facilities are often barred on account of age to children well able to profit from such an experience. Several of the other children in this group were also interested in chess and were unlikely to find in their own age group children with whom they could play. Some played with their parents; other parents admitted that they were already no match for their children. It seems unfortunate that in many schools use of the school library and access to recreational activities is limited to children within certain age groups or stages in the school, when there may well be much younger children in the school who would wish to participate and who would have sufficiently developed interest to profit from the experience. There is a tendency for some schools to be unnecessarily restrictive in what they offer because their expectations of the range of skills and interests is based too closely on an age criterion. Several children in this group who were less fortunate in the stimulation and reading materials which their homes could offer at this later stage suffered a limit to their development for which the schools could have helped to compensate. The children on whom the teachers tended to comment favourably with regard to their wide interests in reading were those for whom the homes had managed to provide progressively wider and more stimulating materials and experiences. This had clearly resulted in these children having a wide range of experiences to contribute to discussions in the classroom and to their own written work.

Thus in general these children were successful in school, many in oral as well as in written work and in arithmetic as well as in language. As a group they seemed popular with other children and many were leaders. Their reading interests were wide and they seemed to be regarded as stimulating to both other children and the teachers. Few negative comments were made by the teachers, who it should be remembered had no part in referring the children to the study and could well have resented them having been singled out for special attention. The average or below average motor co-ordination which affected the written work of some of the group did not seem to be sufficiently poor to prevent their being acceptable to other children though several of the boys were described as awkward or slow in games or timid in physical education.

Parent Contact with the School

On the forms referred to above the head teacher and class teacher were both also asked questions concerning parental contact with the school. The child's present teacher was answering the questions with regard to the past year, or even less, during which the child had been in her class; the head teacher was usually replying in connection with approaches to the school over several years – except where the head teacher had changed or the child had moved to a new school. Because of the presence of the fluent reader in the research there had of necessity been some contact between the parents and the head-teacher as the referral to the university had come from the school in the first instance and the original class teacher or head teacher had approached the parents for their co-operation. Thus neither the type of contact nor the extent found in this study are necessarily typical of an unselected group of such children; nor indeed is the amount of special attention which the children received in school. As mentioned earlier, the present class teacher had not been involved in the initial referral and there had been no contact with the school or the children during the previous year. It therefore seemed valuable to have some idea of the extent of contact between the present class teacher and the parents as seen by the teacher, especially in view of the extreme reluctance in approaching the school as described by some of the parents. It also seemed valuable to determine whether there had been frequent visits by the parents to the head teacher and also whether visits paid by the parents were regarded by the teachers as excessive.

The questions asked of both class teacher and head teacher were: 'Has his/her mother written or discussed any problems with you? YES/NO. If Yes, please indicate frequency and problems' (similarly for father).

The answers to these questions confirmed the impression gained from the parents themselves that they seldom visited the school to discuss problems or wrote either to the class teacher or to the head teacher. The parents had required to contact their children's earlier teacher to obtain permission for absence when visiting the university for testing. At the time of this enquiry when all the children had been in school for at least a year, few of the parents had approached either the class teacher or the head teacher to discuss any problems. None was reported as a parent 'over-concerned' with his or her child's progress. Contacts with fathers tended to have been on 'open nights' or parents' days when a general invitation had been issued to all parents. A few mothers had in addition visited the school about 'particular' problems, for example where a child was tearful and unsettled and unwilling to go to school, or in one instance when the child was distressed at the prospect of a change of school; in an 'ita' school it was felt the child was being confused by being asked to read 'ita'; or where after the father's death a child was distressed at leaving the mother. Generally the parents did not visit the school except on invitation either to talk to the head teacher or class teacher. Where the class teachers mentioned having discussed a child's progress with the mother, they tended to have met casually at the shops or in the street.

This information confirms the impression gained from the parents at the second interview when many showed diffidence at the thought of contacting the school uninvited, feeling that they would be thought to be expecting excessive time or attention to be spent on their children. It should not be taken to mean that these parents were not vitally interested in their children's progress nor even that they would not have welcomed more contact with and information from the school. They were, however, almost embarrassed by their children's success and did not wish to appear to be asking for exceptional treatment. Their appreciation that the teacher was a busy professional was the explanation for this limited contact.

Some of the children in this study were not only precocious in reading development but were also highly gifted intellectually. It is a tribute to their parents and to their teachers that they were developing successfully without becoming unacceptable socially either to adults or to other children. So much attention is focused on able misfits (Kellmer Pringle 1970) and the likely imbalance in the development of the 'bookish' child that it seems important to stress the normality of these children as seen by not only their parents but also by their school. Many showed their exceptionality in school to a much greater extent when allowed a choice of topic rather than a more limited class activity. It is important to ensure that children like these as well as others are not only helped but encouraged to develop their originality in school as well as outside. A narrow curriculum or constraints on acceptable answers or layout may well cramp the development of some of the outstanding qualities in such children – especially where the home may not have the skills or knowledge to compensate. Not all teachers can accept a child who is brighter than she is, and who already at seven years of age is more knowledgeable on a wide variety of subjects. A wide technical knowledge on a variety of subjects was already possessed by some of the children in this study. Most of such children would meet at some time, if they had not already done so, a teacher who saw them as a threat to her authority and who resented their greater knowledge or enquiring nature. It is to be hoped that in general their education would provide them with an extension of the experiences for which so many of them had acquired the foundations within their own homes and that where the home could no longer provide a sufficient stimulation the school would then ensure that the initial impetus was

retained. Some of the group were of course not outstanding intellectually and it is equally important that neither the home nor the
school should set expectations for these children beyond their
capacity either because of their precocious start or because of their
involvement in this research.

Samples of the children's written work were enclosed by some
teachers, some sending only written English, others jotters also containing arithmetic. School jotters were brought on request by a
number of the parents when attending for interview a few months
after the completed reports were received from the schools. These
samples provided confirmation of the high or very high marks
obtained by the children generally in their written work. It was
difficult to assess the breadth of the written work of which some of
the children were capable where the samples included only insertion
of the appropriate word in sentences copied from workbooks or the
blackboard. Some teachers enclosed sample compositions as examples
of the level of free written work of which the child was capable,
indicating the context in which the work had been set, whether that
topic was set to the whole class or whether there was free choice and
whether it was based on prior discussion or reading. Some of these
compositions showed not only or even necessarily greater length
than would have been expected of a child of their age. Many did,
however, show a feel for the style of written language unusual at
their age, a precision of vocabulary and of appropriate written syntax which was remarkable. For some, writing was clearly already at
this stage far removed from speech written down. This point will be
developed further in the following chapter in the context of the
children's reading interests as obtained from the diaries they kept for
a period of a month and in relation to their oral language during
interview.

Several of the written samples showed not only the high level of
performance with regard to content and spelling to which the
teachers had referred, but also the average or below average standard of handwriting. It is pertinent to consider whether the quality
of handwriting was generally average or below or whether this was
particularly evident in compositions where the children were trying,
often at a first attempt, to produce graphic appropriate and con-
tinuous narrative. It seems important to separate these aspects and
to relate quality of presentation of written work to the child's priori-
ties in the task in hand. Certainly some of these children were producing accurate work of poor written appearance and where they
were quick in working as well as accurate it might well have been
appropriate to use strategies to encourage them to take a greater

pride in the appearance of their work. It should be noted that for some poor fine motor co-ordination was probably the cause of their difficulties and that as they matured their work would improve in standard. Others could have been helped by an analysis of the features leading to illegibility of handwriting. For example several were failing to leave sufficient space between words which, in addition to detracting from its appearance, made it more difficult to read. None of the children, even those whose handwriting was of poor quality, made spelling errors. Thus it was unlikely that general carelessness was an adequate or even an appropriate explanation. This is not the place for a lengthy discussion of the techniques for improving legibility of handwriting but there are a number of readily available sources of such information. The crucial point, however, is the specificity of the causes of illegibility in any person's writing which would require attention in order to improve its quality. In short, for some of these children the quality of their writing would improve with age and improved fine motor co-ordination; others could have been assisted by guidance in a framework of written productions (for advice with regard to left-handed children see Clark 1974, pp. 30–44).

With regard to handwriting and also style in composition, a standard of production is often required of children which is seldom attained by, or expected of adults. Children such as these, who were clearly skilled at and interested in variations in the written language for different purposes, could well have been encouraged to evaluate and improve not only the appearance, but the content of their written work. Clearly there is a place for spontaneity in some types of written work; in others even adults draft and redraft to improve the precision of meaning for which they are searching. Some of these children are certainly well able to make their own critical evaluation of their written work to improve the style with rewriting and to write in different styles for different purposes. It seems important to capitalize on the strengths of these children, which includes their sensitivity to the weaknesses in their own work, and to ensure not only that there is a purpose in the written work set for them but also that the child is himself aware of the purpose. The role of drafts in written work and of attention to the preceding phrases and sentences in determining the appropriate succeeding ones, as discussed by Britton, is pertinent with some children with the skills evidenced here if their early sensitivity to the characteristics of print is to be developed and capitalized upon in the school context (Britton 1975).

The breadth of their reading interests as well as their early start in developing these are valuable assets. The role this plays in supplying children with interesting information and stimulating conversation in the oral language interaction in school *and* in the development of a lucid and precise style of written language is perhaps insufficiently appreciated. Children with prolonged difficulties in reading, even if these are ultimately remediated, will have suffered an incalculable and often unrecognized disadvantage in the development of their own written language; while on the contrary, children such as those in the present study will already at seven or eight years of age not only have mastered the concepts of print but also already have developed a feel for the characteristics of a variety of styles of written language on which they can capitalize in producing their own stories and reports. They will not necessarily simulate the style of any particular author, though indeed this they may do at times, but they are likely to synthesize and adapt styles to suit their purposes provided they are placed in situations in which they can capitalize on these experiences and develop the skills. The reason for this emphasis should become clearer with discussion of these children's reading and related experiences which were a background to their school performance. The relevance of the comment by the teacher who observed that the fluent reader in her class showed his skills to the greatest advantage when writing on topics of his own choosing should now be apparent.

In the following chapter the inter-relatedness of school and home experiences in determining the interests, variety and quality of work produced by children in school will it is hoped also become apparent.

CHAPTER VII

Reading and Other Interests a Few Years On

All the children were sent a diary for Christmas and asked to keep a record for the month of January 1973 of all the books they read. This was shortly after the reports discussed in the previous chapter were received from the schools. They were asked to return the relevant pages at the end of the month. Most completed the pages themselves, a few of the younger children tired of the task before the end of the month and the diary was returned incomplete or completed by one of the parents. While this strategy for finding out their range of reading had limitations, it did give some valuable information on the variety and extent of reading, although the children did not always give sufficient detail to identify all the books. It was also helpful as a starting point for the interviews with the children which were held in March 1973. January was the month chosen for several reasons. One was that it was hoped it would appeal to the children to receive an 'office' type diary at the correct time and that they would therefore be more likely to complete it in the first impetus after receiving it. January was on the other hand probably an atypical month as far as reading material was concerned since the children would receive a number of books as presents and these might not necessarily be their own choice. It could also be argued that the very presence of a diary to be completed might increase the children's reading during that month or that they might have been encouraged to finish or indeed to tackle more books than was normal. Though indeed these points must be taken into account, it should be remembered that interviews with parents and children were held only a few months later and during both interviews the children's interests in books and other related activities were discussed.

The families were invited to come back for a visit to the department which had moved to a new building since the earlier interviews, during which a promise had been made to bring them back later. As mentioned earlier, all but three families attended, two of these had left the district, the third was the family whose interview had taken place in school at the earlier stage. This family, who did not reply to the invitation, were not sent a reminder as it was known that the father was shy of such a visit. They had, however, kept contact and the diary had been returned with a covering letter from the father saying that he took his daughter to the library twice a week and that in addition she read a variety of daily papers. He also read one story a week from the paper to her – the rest she read herself. Thus contact was maintained with the complete group of children seen when they started school – except for those who left the district.

The final interviews of the parents were all carried out by the author while a former student who had no prior contact with the children was responsible for the interviews with the children. The aim of these latter interviews was to obtain as much information as possible on the present range of interests of these children – the youngest of whom was barely six while the oldest were about nine years of age. Because of the age range, a variety of material was available in the interview room to act as a focus for discussion. With some of the shyer children this was important in order to reassure them, and with some of the less vocal it also helped where they were inclined to give monosyllabic answers. This was, however, a problem with only a very small minority; most enjoyed the interview and extended it themselves spontaneously.

In the earlier interviews, when the children had recently started school, many parents mentioned their children's interest in the daily papers and also that the children themselves looked up the times of the television programmes they wished to watch. A wide range of daily papers, comics and television journals was therefore made available. During the interview the children were asked which papers if any they read and which parts they found interesting. It was possible for the interviewer to assess the children's familiarity with the papers by observing the way they handled them and their presence also helped to make for a more relaxed interview. It had also appeared from the earlier interview that many were interested not only in newspapers and sources of information on television programmes but also in maps and atlases. A number of maps were also made available during the interview including a copy of the map of central Glasgow which had been sent to the parents to assist them in finding the department. The children were asked to try and find how to trace their route; it was also possible to note if the children were aware of the scale of the map and that they would not find their home on such a map.

The diary entries were used as a focus for the initial questions when the children's interest in books was discussed. They were also asked to select a story they had read and to tell the beginning into a tape-recorder in such a way as to interest another child in reading it. It was hoped that by formalizing the situation in this way the children would be led to use 'book-type' language rather than the more conversational style of the rest of the interview. It has been noted by the author in another study that even pre-school children if read a story several times will in retelling frequently adopt the style of the author and simulate his language even when they do not remember the actual words. It was hoped that these children would give the flavour of the author. Some children did, while some obviously felt that if they were trying to interest another child they should describe the story in colloquial terms. Although some interesting examples emerged, the strategy was not as successful as had been hoped. The children were perhaps too old and therefore rather self-conscious in this task. One or two of the younger children did as the pre-school children and changed both their language and intonation when apparently reading from the book, and any asides to the interviewer were in a different, more conversational style.

Other topics discussed were the children's favourite games and the extent to which these involved other children, their views on school and their likes and dislikes in the school day. Finally, in an attempt to elicit imaginative responses, they were given as copies for drawing the situations in de Bono's *Children Solve Problems* (de Bono, 1972). The children were given paper and coloured pens and asked to draw solutions to problems such as the following:

1. Show how you would stop a cat and a dog from fighting.
2. Design a fun machine.
3. If you were the Zoo Keeper and wanted to find out how heavy an elephant was, how would you do it?
4. If you wanted to build a house more quickly, how would you do it?
5. Draw a picture showing how you could make your body better.
6. If you were a policeman how would you deal with bad men?
7. Design a special bicycle for a postman.
8. Design a special bed for people who have difficulty in going to sleep.
9. Design a space rocket in which astronauts could live on the moon for three weeks.

As the children's comments and explanations are often as important as the actual drawings these were noted in full.

All the interviews were taped and notes were made under the main topic headings by the interviewer who had not met the children previously and who had only limited knowledge of their background in as far as this was necessary to avoid embarrassing the children by questions. As many illustrative comments as possible were transcribed in the children's own language. With the wide age range studied and the variety of material obtained from the interview, it seems best here to group the children by age and to describe the type of information which seemed to vary with age.

1. *Youngest Boys*

Eight of the boys were aged less than seven years of age when the school reports were received. At interview a few months later all these boys had some knowledge of the daily papers and could at least find the television programmes and identify those in which they were interested. The youngest boy in the study gave the following topics as his interests in his particular daily paper – readers' letters, the guide to 'V.A.T.' price changes, the cartoon strips and jokes (a common interest), the news and the football news. One of the others in this group asked the interviewer if she had seen a report of an incident involving a boy who had caused a great deal of trouble – as this had been 'headline news' in the paper he had read at his grandfather's. This boy was also interested in the prices of food as listed in a particular supermarket advertisement, even although it was not the shop his mother used. He said he just found it interesting. Another studied the weather reports and could turn without hesitation to the correct page. For another the timetable of television programmes was of interest; while another was also interested in the football news. The rest clearly dipped into at least one daily paper, including studying the headlines. One boy said he read two papers each day. Their familiarity with daily papers was clear from the way they handled them and could find the relevant pages. Further, they were both willing and able to discuss them intelligently with adults whom they were meeting for the first time. They also had the normal interest in comics of children of their age.

Their television interests were also extensive and included children's programmes and cartoons; several were already showing interest in some of the more adult comic programmes. One who gave a long list of programmes he liked admitted he did not watch them all each week. He also remarked that if he was watching he did not read or do other things at the same time. This was a point made by a number of the parents who, while commenting that viewing was not discouraged, stressed that selectivity was encouraged and that concentrating on one thing at a time was a rule.

Even this youngest group of boys grasped the essential characteristics of a street plan. Some could locate the university on the map, could find the main landmarks and knew that they would not find their home on the available maps, although several had travelled a considerable distance and were relatively unfamiliar with Glasgow and none lived close to the University. Their general knowledge included some appreciation of Glasgow in relation to Scotland – one offered to find Britain on a map of the world and knew the size relationship of Scotland to Britain.

This group in general liked school although several had particular reservations. Examples of some of the comments are as follows:

One boy did not like reading – because the books were 'awful boring'. Another disliked drawing – 'because it makes my arm sore'. To the question 'anything you don't like about school?' one boy replied, 'Well one thing is certain, I don't like hard work!', while another replied to the same question 'I don't like certain kinds of sums' ('why?') 'They are too easy'. One boy had reservations which were confined to playtime because he felt bullied by a bigger boy. A final comment from one six-year-old seems to sum up the attitude of the group that although he enjoyed school he wondered whether it was worth all the time it took up! To quote:

Well I'm rather surprised when I come home from school to see the time it's taken up. Six whole hours – or five and three-quarters. I do like school but I don't like the time it takes up.

Only one of the boys showed conceit about how good he was at school and referred to his abilities frequently during the interviews.

Although the boys did not express particular interest in the sums at school, there are frequent examples in the interviews of their interest in size, time and distance to which they referred with precision – or sometimes joking exaggeration of which they were obviously aware. One referred to his cousin living 20 metres away at a time when transfer to metres from yards was still a matter of the future; another said at school he played with 'ten million people'; another referred to this week's copy of his comic as 1052nd to be published. Perhaps the spirit of the interviews and the context in which number was used can be captured by quoting the commentary by one of the six-year-olds while drawing his machine for weighing elephants:

Let's see, 26 stone, 27 stone, 28, 29, 30, 31 stone . . . I think I know what to draw. Ahem, the elephant – Elephant Scales (while writing this on his picture he said the word to himself) average 43 stone . . . How do you spell average? (was told). This will keep you guessing – now the elephant on the scale. I'll have to do it white on this because it should be grey – unless I do it pink!

Asked to tell about the drawing he continued:

That's the elephant scales average 43 stone and that's the elephant there and he weighs 26 stone 2.

He then observed that one to thirteen are all 'on the same stone and then you are on to a different kind of stone'. Asked who told him this he replied that he had weighed himself on the scales (see illustration below). This particular child, while a fluent reader on

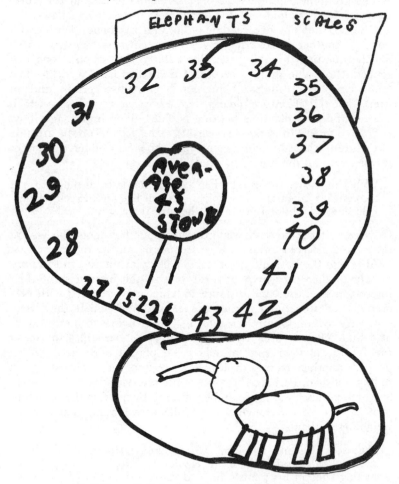

Illustration 1. Scale for Weighing an Elephant – Boy aged 6

starting school, was of average intelligence as measured by the WPPSI, although on the Stanford Binet he was well above average. Neither of his parents had continued into higher education after leaving school; both, however, were concerned to know what the prospects were for their son and wished predictions to be made, predictions which were made all the more difficult by the conflicting results on the intelligence tests. While able to use language appropriately and succinctly he had not an outstanding ability to explain concepts or to define words. His independence of views were evident also in his diary return where he entered not only the books he had received or read but comments indicating where he had obtained the reading material and whether he had liked it, as follows:

> A freind of mum's gave me three volumes of a children's encyclopeadia by Arthur Mee but I don't like them very much.
>
> I went to the library and got a book about speaking French – it was good.
>
> I went to the library and got a French book caulld. Teach Yourself French by N. Scarlyn Wilson. It's about First Lessons in French.

(This was written in capital letters and the spelling is as the original.)

Examples from the interview and diary of this child, who contributed none of the examples quoted earlier, have been given in some detail because this seemed the best way of capturing the flavour of the oral language of the children at this age, their sense of fun, the way in which their speaking, reading and writing are interrelated and the easy way in which they interacted in an interview situation.

In the diaries of the other young boys there was confirming evidence of regular interest in the daily papers, comics, annuals and collections of stories which are often read to children of their age and also of many information books. Kipling, Lewis Carroll and Swift were also beginning to appear in the lists and most of the children had an obvious love for a variety of books by Enid Blyton. One of the boys was in hospital for a short spell which, as his mother indicated, meant that he read more than normal. His mother attached to the diary a list of material he loved to browse through which did not appear on the diary as having been read; these included cookery books, telephone directory, bus timetables, street directories, maps, dictionary. Several other boys were also reported by their parents at interview to find such materials fascinating.

The written comments made by the interviewer in a footnote on one particular boy in this group seem a fitting summary on the group, applying as they do to most of these six-year-olds and not only to the child in question.

His interests in books and in television programmes are a mixture of things appropriate for his age, for example, Teddy Bear Comic, Tom & Jerry on television, and things indicating a desire for knowledge, for example, reading encyclopedias, watching quiz games on television and the daily paper. At present he reconciles the two different levels very well. His manner is that of a child much older than he is, or even an adult at times. It would be easy to forget that he sometimes will do things typical of six-year-olds. Perhaps one of the difficulties of these children is that because they are more advanced in some ways, adults expect them to be advanced all round and to be rather hard on them when they display behaviour actually typical of children of their age.

2. *The Seven-Year-Old Boys*

Six of the boys were between seven and eight years of age when the reports were received. This group showed similarly wide interests but were beginning to show a more mature outlook in their comments. Their interests in reading while still including comics as well as the daily papers also included science fiction, stories about the war and classics such as Robinson Crusoe and Treasure Island – and a book of Burns poetry. One boy said he disliked story books but was interested in different countries, their population and capitals; another commented that his favourites were 'creepy' books and that he liked 'sub-serious' rather than serious stuff. Most of them said they still liked school, although one commented that he was glad he didn't get all the extra sums he had been given previously; another that he felt sums kept him from the library. One child seemed to have conflicting feelings about getting special sums as he had at first, saying he preferred to have the same as the rest instead of special ones as previously, quoting the teacher as saying that they would be revision for him. As he considered this comment he decided he preferred special ones. The underlying conflict was whether and to what extent he wished to be seen as different in order to have stimulating enough work. This same boy mentioned that his father had wanted him to have a better reading book instead of 'Janet and John things' and had sent the teacher a letter, and he was then given *Treasure Island* which he was enjoying!

These children were beginning to show an adult turn of phrase and a wide speaking vocabulary and most were at ease but not over-confident in the interview. Only in one instance did the inter-

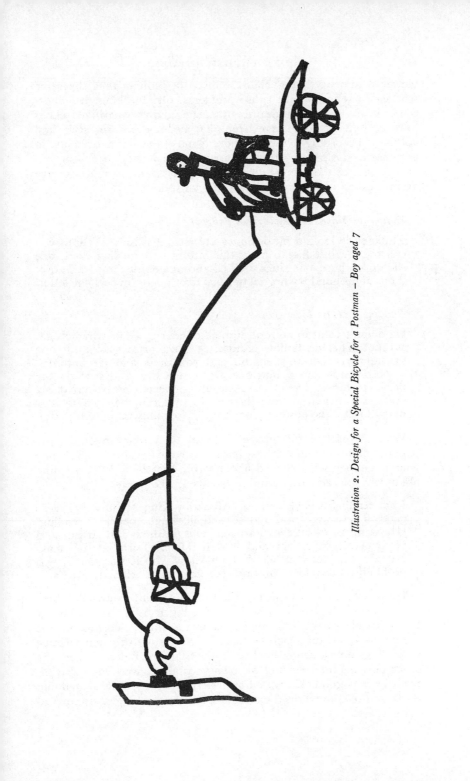

Illustration 2. Design for a Special Bicycle for a Postman — Boy aged 7

viewer comment that a child seemed so familiar that the same manner in school might cause problems. On checking the school report it was found that his present teacher had very positive feelings towards him. It may have been that he modified his style and volubility according to the situation. None of the actual drawings in response to the puzzle situations were particularly outstanding but an example of the commentary which accompanied some will give an impression of the boys' conversational style:

Design for a Special Bicycle for a Postman

The bicycle looks a 'bit ordinary at first but it isn't. Well, as you can see, he just has to press this button – these shoot out, one shoots out here, one rings the bell and one holds the letter, grabs it out of his hand – whiz – letter box door opens, in goes the letter.

Building a House More Quickly

He doesn't want to do it all himself of course, that's why he's got a robot – he has hollow hands . . . the mortar shoots out, the bricks, then mortar sticks on and you press another button – whoosh shoots out a magic trowel inside him and it sticks the bricks together. These wires are all connected and a great big sheet of paper automatically goes in to a roll, telling him how many bricks, the position they are . . . (see illustrations on p. 81).

While several of this group listed in their diary mainly daily papers, comics and annuals, several gave an extensive list. The boy whose comments are quoted above wrote that he enjoyed reading about war and adventure and also comedy. To quote:

I am reading a book entitled 'All about King Arthur.' It is very good. There are one hundred and fifty-eight pages of reading. (He went on to list the characters and finished) But Arthur and his men recovered her and took her to be burnt at the steak. But someone rescued her. I don't know who it was, but it was probbably Lancelot. The End. (spelling as in original)

He was reading *Kidnapped* at the time of the interview and chose it as his story to retell. This child's intelligence on the WPPSI at five years of age was only slightly above average, information was the only sub-test on which he scored high. As with the child in the previous group he scored higher on the Stanford Binet. As with the other boy, his interests and his own vocabulary were high and his memory was good. He was, however, not outstanding at defining words out of context or at explaining concepts in the ways required

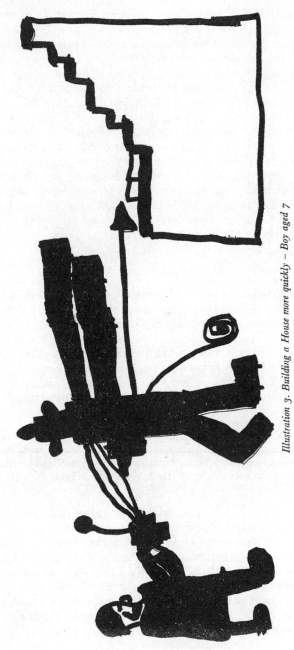

Illustration 3. Building a House more quickly – Boy aged 7

in standardized intelligence tests. It seems important to stress that neither of these boys was from a home where either parent had higher education – nor would a standardized intelligence test have identified the boys as outstanding. It is for this reason that this chapter should be read in conjunction with the earlier one containing the results of the intelligence testing. While details which might identify the precise children are being excluded from this chapter it is hoped that the examples from the diaries, extracts from conversation together with limited background information are enough to give a clear picture of the children. One child's entries in the diary were limited for January because according to his mother, his new hobby of chess was taking up most of his spare time. He did still manage to read a book on chess, books on dangerous animals, car makers, the first animals, inside the earth, into space and the Highway Code. All these books were either from the local library or home. He also listed two school textbooks.

3. Boys of Over Eight Years of Age

The remaining five boys who were between eight and nine years of age when the school reports were received were already showing an adult ability to organize their conversation to supply information to a variety of questions. These five were from a variety of home backgrounds but all had an intelligence quotient of at least 120 on the WPPSI when first tested and of over 140 on the Stanford Binet and are therefore in some ways a special case. A quotation from the interviewer about one of the boys was also true of several others –

> His verbal fluency and facility are quite outstanding. He never made small talk or said anything silly . . . He would go off at tangents or remember something relevant to earlier questions . . . He obviously had a thirst for knowledge which he satisfies by reading.

The information obtained from this group showed a further development of interests similar to those in the younger group.

A greater interest in word games and in chess was developing and in all sources of information whether books, daily papers, television or conversation. As with the others, a drive and enthusiasm for a wide variety of activities was apparent. These boys were as seems normal with boys of that age, less enthusiastic about school, though not actively hostile to attendance. Several made comments about work which was boring because it was too easy. One boy mentioned that he was having some special Latin lessons from the head teacher. His original interest was sparked off by a quotation in Latin in a story book he was reading and his father had managed to find him an old Latin grammar which he was studying himself. His class teacher then asked the head teacher if he would help. Meeting the head teacher some time later the author learned that these lunchtime Latin lessons were found to be mutually enjoyable. This same boy played chess in the school club. Only one of these boys had been promoted to a class with older children and it was he who mentioned several times his dislike of sums and English. He gave as his reason, 'all the writing makes your hand sore'. He was in Group A and said he did not like that because he got reading to do then a 'big summary about that size' (indicating). 'It's horrible, you've got to write it all down.'

Two of these boys were rather shy during the interview and while giving appropriate answers did not expand them spontaneously as had the younger children. When asked to draw the solutions to a 'de Bono' puzzle they tended to give several alternative solutions and to choose to illustrate and comment on several rather than on one. Several of the drawings were in the form of plans with the appropriate parts labelled. Two examples from one boy give some illustration of the type of content.

Special Bed for People Who Have Difficulty in Going to Sleep

This had a bottle containing a sleeping drug dispensed by a tube, a lullaby microphone, a very soft mattress and rocking wheels – and a hammer if all else fails!

A Special Bicycle for a Policeman

This had a machine which dropped hard toffee to give dogs toothache and a bone firer – a steering wheel and high up pedals to protect the legs, and spiked mudguards.

Another eight-year-old's fun machine is illustrated on p. 84.

Thus, these older boys also found this type of problem stimulating and were well aware that originality was being encouraged. Like the others they were self-conscious about the actual drawings.

The books mentioned in the diaries were similar in range to those mentioned by the other groups. Several boys obviously enjoyed reading a number of books by the same author in quick succession, which might also have been apparent with the younger boys had the diaries been kept over a longer period than one month. In addi-

Illustration 4. Design for a Fun Machine – Boy aged 8

tion to information books and a number of classics, Enid Blyton books came in for frequent mention, while Biggles, Billy Bunter and Jennings were also mentioned.

4. *The Girls a Few Years Later*

All the girls but one interviewed in 1973 were aged seven or eight years of age at the time of the school reports. The remaining girl who was six years of age was the only girl referred to the study as a fluent reader on the second request to schools – while eight boys were referred at that time. The younger boys were much more spontaneous and enthusiastic in the interview situation than the older boys and their contributions were therefore quoted in some detail at the beginning of this chapter to set the scene for the rest of the discussion. Unfortunately the girls did not seem to find either the interview or the drawing situation one to which they responded readily or fluently. Although not apparently unhappy during the interview they tended to give minimum answers and to be unwilling to expand on further questioning. Even the drawing situation did not stimulate them to unusual or creative responses and they seemed at least as self-conscious as the boys about the inadequacy of the actual drawings. The commentaries to the drawings were mainly not only limited but conventional. While this does not of course mean that some other situation might not have elicited more creative or qualitatively interesting dialogue, these types of responses to a creativity task are however in line with the dichotomy found by Hutt in longitudinal comparisons of sex differences in creativity. Boys were found to give significantly more original responses (Hutt 1972) and (Hutt and Bhavnani 1972). In the light of the limited nature of the material obtained, its similarity across the two age groups of seven and eight-year-olds, and the fact that there was only one six-year-old who was particularly inhibited and shy during interview, it was decided to report on the ten girls in a single section and draw attention to any exceptions to the general pattern. Even the story-telling situation stimulated only a few; one girl parried the interviewer's requests with a succession of excuses as to why she could not retell a story while another only agreed on condition the tape-recorder was switched off.

The interviews did not provide much additional information about the girls except to confirm that they were settled, acceptable children, happy at school with the normal range of interests and activities for girls of their age. As with the boys they could understand the map and did consult the daily papers for information on television programmes at least. They liked school but were shy of expressing particular likes and dislikes of particular aspects of the school day. It was learned from the second interview with the parents that at least two of the girls played chess, that one organized a lending library with her sister and that another went up to her room alone where she had been heard either reading or telling stories. None of this sort of information was elicited from the children themselves, who talked of playing with their friends. Whether the girls were projecting the image of themselves they thought to be expected it is hard to say. It is interesting to note that one mother did assure me at interview that in spite of the fact that her daughter had read early she was normal in her interests for a girl of her age and that she did not have to make her put down her books. It would appear subjectively that many of these children were reaching an age when boys rather than girls begin to be critical of school and the very fact that these girls were contented in school and ready to accept what was offered could be one reason for lack of detail on that aspect.

The diaries which were returned by the girls showed a rather different choice of books from those which were reported by the boys. Books of fairy tales including Anderson and Grimm were mentioned, a large number of Enid Blyton mystery books for girls were mentioned by most; books on horses, ballet and on wild flowers were all mentioned. The classics mentioned included *Little Women, Black Beauty, The Water Babies, Alice in Wonderland, Treasure Island* and *Swallows and Amazons*. Several of the girls, in addition to listing the books, supplied comments on whether and why they had enjoyed particular books; one girl aged eight, who noted the Bible as regular reading, also mentioned *Jane Eyre*. She also included on the 'Notes' page a list of books she would like to read complete with authors, all correctly spelt. Among these were *The Three Musketeers, Pride and Prejudice* and *Heidi Grows Up*. This particular girl was already outstanding in school at five years of age by her concern for right and wrong and her mature outlook combined with a sensitivity which led her to become distressed at injustice or cruelty. Her first teacher had been very sensitive to the needs of this child, as well as encouraging her reading interests. This was confirmed by the parents who reported that the teacher had encouraged her to join the library. She was one of the few girls who responded to the story-telling or to the drawing situations. The other girl who responded at any length to these situations punctuated her drawings with a running commentary as she drew a bicycle for a policeman. This same girl enjoyed telling a story, selecting an Enid Blyton story which she told at great length, capturing precisely the style of her favourite author (an extract will be quoted later). She also reported that she loved writing stories herself – mystery stories of twenty or thirty pages. She was the girl who was reported as enjoying reading aloud to herself. This is perhaps why she was so much at home in this oral presentation of a story, since she obviously appreciated the spoken language of books as having a particular dimension of its own.

5. *The Children and the Language of Books*

The continuing interest in books as in a wide range of other activities was apparent from the information obtained from the interviews and the diaries completed by the children. Before turning to consider the parents' perception of their children as reported in the final interview, it would seem valuable to give some examples from the story-telling and written work of the children at this stage. In the story-telling situation, unfortunately, the instructions were perhaps not specific enough. As they were open to different interpretations some children, in order to tempt a friend to read the book, used a colloquial or conversational style. This tended to be true if they tried to retell the salient points in the story. Others tried to capture the opening sections in the language of the author. The following are extracts from some of these to show the variety of styles adopted,

Boy aged seven
One day Parsley was taking a quiet stroll through the park . . .

Girl aged seven
. . . Suddenly through the little dirty window at the door there came a sound. 'Psst.' It was Joe. 'I've come to rescue you,' she whispered. 'Joe you are a wonder,' said Julian . . . (This style was continued at length)

Boy aged eight
He went into the most comfortable room in the club and said, 'Fishing', he muttered. 'Fishing, I'm going fishing in the French mountains . . .'

Girl aged eight
. . . Jean laughed and went on her way. But the little man was right, before long her memory had fallen out . . .

As can be seen even from the extracts above, the children used a language different from normal conversational speech. They used a different vocabulary, a more elaborate syntax, inversion and variety of conjunctions, and made frequent use of direct, rather than reported speech. An interesting contrast is the child from whom an abstract is now quoted who chose colloquial speech for this situation. The book he had recently enjoyed was *Tom Sawyer* and his report was:

A am gonnie tell ye aboot the fust bit o' Tom Sawyer. His aun'ie seen that he had jam roon his mooth an' she thought he had eat'n fae the jam pot . . .

Although this transcript may be understandable to other than Glaswegians, it is unlikely that the tape-recording would be! This does not mean, however, that this boy did not enjoy the book – or appreciated it any the less. The fact that he used colloquial speech for oral communication did not mean that in written work he failed to transfer to a register, syntax and vocabulary more appropriate for that. *While still retaining his colloquial language in speech he had learned to read fluently with understanding and appreciation and at an early age.* Through this contact with a wide range of books, he was now learning to produce a written style very different from his speech. Although he had not yet mastered the appropriate punctuation, the actual language is that of written communication, and very different from the example above, as can be seen from the extract given below:

Alone

Once I was on a desert island I had been shipwrecked I awoke to find that I was on an island. I went to fish I caught one and went home to a hut made of twigs which I made earlier . . . I ripped the sleeve off of it and tied it on to the stick with the string I used for fishing . . . (spelling as in the original).

Although no punctuation was used, the sentences were quite clear, the tenses were varied appropriately and there was only one use of an expression which he might have used orally but which was inappropriate in written language, namely 'I seen' instead of 'I saw'.

Further extracts from written work sent by teachers of four other boys will also be quoted to illustrate the development from a mixture of written language and 'speech written down' to a style of written language. (All spelling and punctuation are as in the original.)

1. *Boy aged 6*

When the astonauts arrived on the moon they went for a moon drive. They have a special car called a moon buggy. It is a little car with small wheels. It is not like mummies car at all. The astronauts used the moon buggy to explore the moon. They found some rocks and put them in the rocket when they tried to pick up the rocks they were like drunk men and they nearly floated away because there is no air on the moon.
THE END.

2. *Boy aged almost 7*

The Vikings

They were fierce warriors. They lived nearly 1,000 years ago. They came from Norway, Denmark and Sweden, which are

Scandinavian countries. For protection they had shelds, battle-axes spears, swords and helmets . . .

3. *Boy aged 8*
   Three Wishes
   Last night I was looking at a picture of an extinct bird when suddenly the bird spoke to me and said that I could have three wishes. My first wish was that the reservoirs would never run dry. My second wish was that I could go forward in time to the year 5000 . . .

4. *Boy aged 8*
   My Dream
   I went to bed. Well, at least I thought so! I was so dreamy that night! When I woke up I was in what you might term 'Dream-land'. I dreamt I was world chess champion Bobby Fischer! I was playing chess with George Best and I had just taken a pawn while defending my bishop . . .

Samples of written work were sent from the schools for only a limited number of the children and in most instances there was only a single composition. None the less, the examples given above show the way in which, with the assistance of their early fluent reading and interest in a wide range of books over a few years, they were developing a style of written language. It would have been interesting to analyse the extent to which they were already capable of varying their style for different types of written communication but this was not possible from the examples available.

When the information in this chapter is taken in conjunction with the details of the children in school as described in the previous chapter it is clear that many of these children did maintain their early promise. The extracts from their conversation and their written work when combined with their breadth of interests, perhaps shows why so many are regarded as stimulating and amusing companions by adults and children alike. In the following chapter the picture will be completed with some of the additional information obtained from the parents in the final interview and their perception of their children a few years after starting school.

CHAPTER VIII

Now and Then as Seen by a Parent

The second interview of one or both parents took place in the university at the same time as the interviews of the children described in the previous chapter. Indeed a number of the topics were discussed both with the parents and the children including the range of reading interests and access to books, television viewing, progress at and interest in school. Further information was also obtained about pre-school experiences, confirming much of the earlier information which could now in some cases be amplified by comparisons with siblings who had reached school age and whose attitude to books and approach to learning to read could be compared with the fluent reader in this study. All these interviews which were carried out by the author were taped and later transcribed and summarized by a student who had not been involved in the earlier part of the study.

Where any comments by parents amplified the earlier information, or was relevant to the children's interests or to the school progress this has been incorporated in the appropriate earlier chapters. In this present chapter some of the observations by the parents and their comparisons between the children's present and previous interests will be separately reported.

Books and Other Interests

The parents confirmed the interest in a wide range of reading as indicated in the children's diaries. The parents of the girls tended to emphasize an interest in a wide range of stories as found in the diaries though a few mentioned non-fiction in addition. Two girls were reported to be writing themselves; one wrote plays and poems, the other stories. Another (as mentioned earlier) enjoyed reading books aloud to herself; while yet another in collaboration with her sister ran their own lending library. The parents did not give a picture of the girls as absorbed in books to the exclusion of all else – or as preferring books to the company of other children. Most of the girls obtained some of their books from the local library although several of those who had elder sisters were said to have an ample supply of books in the house. Several parents reported an early interest in reading by another child in the family.

The boys almost without exception were also reported as using the local library and the few who did not lived too far away. Most went to the library regularly, and on their own. One boy was reported to have been given an adult ticket by the librarian because of his interests. Many of the parents themselves used the library although they did not necessarily accompany their children and it is important to note the part played by the library in catering for the reading interests of these children from an early age and those of other members of the family. Most of the boys, even the youngest, were interested in non-fiction as well as fiction; though a few only read non-fiction; these latter children were the most difficult to satisfy. Several parents had either purchased encyclopedias or were in the process of doing so. One problem apart from the considerable outlay of money on such purchases was the fact that many of the boys were particularly interested in topics on which the information is quickly dated. A number of libraries did provide resources for such children, but in some libraries these books were in the adult section to which the child still did not have access; while in other libraries they were for reference only and could not be taken out of the library which the parents found was not the most suitable place to study such books. The children wanted to 'browse' for hours with reference books in their own home rather than to 'consult' them in the library. One problem in consulting reference books only in the library would be that the children could not discuss the information as they obtained it. As the regulations governing numbers of tickets allowed to a child, access to the adult section and availability of reference books all varied with different libraries it is perhaps worth considering the reason in a given library for its particular rules and whether and under what conditions exceptions should be permitted. Many of these children were already visiting the library at a very early age, even pre-school, either on their own or on a parent's ticket; now there was evidence of their continuing use of the library on their own initiative. The original visits to the library had in most cases been on the suggestion of and in the company of a parent, though at least two children went on the advice of the school, and one on his own. This latter boy came from a home where both parents enjoyed reading and where the mother described them as sometimes reading quietly for hours as a family. The mother did not obtain her books from the local library but rather by obtaining access to a library in the building in which she worked part-time in an unskilled capacity. While most children used the local libraries and obtained appropriate and interesting reading material themselves, one parent described her son as going to the library and bringing home a number of books which he seldom finished and which she felt he chose by size and colour. The other members in this particular family were not reported as having interest in books and the boy in question had a very high level of reading accuracy combined with an average level of comprehension. This is an instance where further help from the school and the library would have been valuable to capitalize on this child's potential.

While most of the siblings were also felt to be interested in books they were not described as absorbed in the same way as the child in this study. The parents still in this later interview found it difficult, as they had earlier, to give any clear-cut ways in which the child in this study differed from the others. Where there was only one sibling this was superficially easier but no aspect was clearly apparent in the larger families which set this particular child as different – at least in a way which was consistently described across families. While several of the children were described as having a phenomenal memory for minute detail, as mentioned earlier, at least one parent stated that the child's brother had a better memory for certain kinds of detail than the fluent reader. The other siblings did tend to be described as 'more outgoing', more adaptable but also 'more demanding', and the fluent reader as having a dislike of noise 'quieter', 'placid', 'needs some time alone each day, otherwise likes to be with other people'. One parent said that while the sister always *asked* questions the fluent reader always *knew* answers. This parent was referring to family outings where both girls from an early age were interested in all around them and the sibling would ask questions – it would then be apparent that the other child had already understood the implications by herself. An example given was the meaning of a particular ambiguous advertisement which used a play on words. 'Total concentration', 'loses himself completely in what he is doing', 'engrossed', were all terms used of fluent readers by parents, while it was felt that the siblings had more need of the company of others. Comments such as these were made by some parents when referring to the children at the pre-school stage; it was felt that this was perhaps merely because they could already read and therefore to the parent appeared more absorbed or readily occupied. They stressed this power of concentration again at this later date and it should be noted that such comments were frequently also made by the teachers in the school reports.

The parents had found difficulty earlier in describing how the

fluent reader had learnt to read. Some further insight was obtained
at this second interview when parents were comparing the process
of learning to read of the early fluent readers and their siblings who
learnt to read at school. They stressed how different was the
approach of the children. One mother commented of a pre-school
sibling that he did not seem to realize that you must look at the
print when reading rather than the pictures; several mentioned that
the younger sibling was beginning to make the sounds of the letters
and work out words which the other child who read early had
never done – or 'was just pronouncing words like a child' while for
the fluent reader 'it just clicked'. It did seem there was something
qualitatively different in the early reading behaviour of the pre-
school readers and some of the siblings who learnt to read at school.
What one cannot determine from this study is whether this was
because the approaches to learning to read used in the particular
schools were probably more phonically than language based in the
early stages. This difference in approach to the printed word was
stressed by parents even where the siblings were described also as
'good' readers. At least one parent felt that the presence in the
family of an older child who had been so effortlessly successful in
learning to read resulted in the next child being less interested in
reading or discouraged. One sibling who was good at school was
rather unhappy about this for a time saying it was lonely at the top –
an isolation which might not so concern the more self-sufficient fluent
reader.

Home Background

At the time of the initial interview few of the mothers were working
more than part-time, the work normally being chosen to fit in with
the family's needs. This was still true. Several of the mothers were
teaching but even one of these had only a temporary appointment
so that she could give it up without warning if any of the children
were ill; another, although a highly qualified scientist, was working
only a few hours per week. Many encouraged their children to come
home from school at lunch-time. It is not suggested that in order to
provide stimulation for their families it is necessary for all mothers
to stay at home rather than work. In the present climate it is, however, perhaps worth stressing that these parents found this absorption
in their family a satisfying role – even although a few felt guilty at
staying at home. One mother, asked if she would go to work, replied,
'Not if I could help it – I'm trying to balance if it is sheer laziness.'
The following were some of the replies given by mothers when

asked whether they were now out working: 'No, I get guilty feelings,' 'I feel I ought to, so many people do.' They all seemed to regard their lives as active and stimulating and certainly did not feel they were at home from a sense of duty. The expression 'a close-knit family' and 'we delight in having them' were comments made at this interview and continued to echo the kind of remarks made when the children were just starting school and which were also given then as an explanation for not seeking out nursery school provision for their children.

One mother said she would not have sent her children to nursery school because she liked to see what they were doing; another, 'They are OK in poorer areas – I'm not all that keen on them', while another said, 'They can amuse themselves – if you are sort of half-educated!' Their child's dislike of noise was mentioned in other contexts by several mothers and one also commented that her son disliked the noise at nursery school. Another mother who had thought her son enjoyed nursery school was astonished when he commented on his last day, 'Well thank goodness I don't have to go there again!' In contrast, a mother who lived in a high flat regarded the nursery school as a tremendously important part of their lives. 'I'm a great believer in it.'

While there was evidence both from the mothers' attitude to work and to nursery school attendance that they were absorbed in their families, it would be quite misleading to suggest that they were absorbed in their families to the exclusion of all else – or to paint a picture of over-dependent children tied to their parents' apron strings. Clearly many of the mothers, while having ample time to spend with their children, also read widely themselves and led an active life; a combination which they felt would not have been possible had they worked part-time or full-time. Time to read to their children, talk to them *and* listen to them seemed important – though several mothers used the word 'laziness' to excuse themselves. These families, while forming in some instances close-knit units, did not give the impression of discouraging independence on the part of the children if one considers the early age at which the children went to the library on their own, or if this was not possible at least chose their own books; and the encouragement of the children to select their television viewing – though at least one parent did forbid certain programmes to the child who was still in the youngest group. Fathers were described as learning to play chess in order to play with their sons, or the family was described as playing other board games together, while in some families sharing of library books was common. Sometimes the child read the mother or father's book and sometimes the parent read the child's – although one mother stressed how totally different her taste in books was from that of her son. A sense of humour and of fun was mentioned repeatedly and several of the boys were reported to have a skill as mimics. The sense of humour was adult, or could be at a level which adults could appreciate. This was also mentioned by several of the teachers. One boy who was described at school as completely lacking in a sense of humour was described on the contrary by his parents as having a very good sense of humour and as a mimic. Play on words seemed to appeal particularly to many of the boys; this was evident from the description of the television programmes which were now beginning to appeal to them and from the parents' other comments.

The Child in School

In an earlier chapter the children's attainment at school and their adjustment as seen by their teachers was discussed. The views of the children themselves were also obtained. When asked about school at this interview few of the parents said their child actively disliked school; several did comment that the child was bored. One said the child was 'fed up' with his present homework and that he had done it so often that he did not do it well as a protest; another said her son 'wasn't stretched' and as a result his work was not good. Now that he had a more experienced teacher he was more stimulated and therefore producing much better work. Another mother described how her son had been checked for reading books he had brought from home and for doing sum cards of a higher level than he should; while another mother was worried that her son was getting the wrong impression of school because everything was so easy; another was concerned because her son was getting 'lines' to write almost every night, which she thought were for talking, and since he was still managing the work of the class with ease, she wondered if it was because he had not enough to do. Several parents while saying that the child was happy enough at school felt they were not getting on fast enough. They were well aware of their child's potential and it was not felt that these parents wished to 'push' their child or even to push their child at the expense of others. From the reports from school it was clear that the children's work was acceptable, that they were felt to be fitting in with other children, and in the classroom, but it was also noted that few of the parents made contact with the school. It is perhaps important to stress for this reason that some of the children who did make mistakes were felt by their parents to be doing so because the work was too easy and did not stretch them sufficiently; even those who were getting very high marks were felt at least with some teachers not to be given scope to show the real level of their capacities. One child who was restless in school and rather distractable was unfortunately felt to have been influenced by his presence in the research. This mother classified him as bored at school (and indeed at home) saying that her son had claimed 'I'm brainy, I know everything', and wanting to leave school. It is unfortunate if his presence in the research influenced him in this way, it is also sad if this boy's potential is not developed to its limits as he was found at interview to be lively and able to become absorbed in certain activities. Several parents made interesting comments about school work, including a comment that a child's writing was poor because he couldn't write as quickly as he could think – also that her son was more interested in reading than sums at school because large numbers interested him, not the small ones in short sums. Another mother made reference to her son's refusal to write anything he could not spell and commented that the teacher wanted him to do it phonically. Other parents also commented that their child seldom made a spelling error. This was borne out by the written examples which were sent from school.

The objectivity with which the parents could report on their own child and on the school situation was indeed impressive. They clearly had a respect for education and for what the school could offer but also a longing to know more than they did about what was happening in school and also for more contact than was possible at 'open' days. One mother said in a rather surprised voice, 'Teachers don't seem to mind you going up', while another said, 'I would like to go up but they might not be happy about it', while another who had tried said, 'I would like to go sometimes but they don't seem to encourage it'. Yet another felt the teacher might react by, 'Does she think her boy's any better than anyone else's?' It seems sad that with such potential for co-operation the constraints within which the formal educational system works should militate against education being seen as a partnership. The class size and the very framework of the school day, quite apart from the school as an institution, seem to result in 'remote' contact in a formalized setting. Those teachers and parents who had happened to have informal contact in the street or at the shops had obviously enjoyed this and appreciated the greater insight it had provided – such contacts were, however, rare and for only a few children.

Because in most cases the parent interviewed on both occasions was the mother, her role in the children's development has come out more clearly than that of the father although reference was made in

the interviews to the father and questions were asked quite specifically, directed at eliciting information about the extent to which the
father read to the child, read himself, was involved in family outings
and so on. As the information has been analysed it has become
increasingly clear that in most of the homes both parents played a
crucial role in their children's intellectual development and that a
number of the boys particularly were already modelling their speech
and their interests on those of their father. Some of the fathers were
attempting to learn new skills stimulated by the enthusiasm of their
children. It is now a matter of regret that an attempt was not made
to interview all the fathers in order to obtain first-hand confirmation
on their role and their impressions of their family.

It is perhaps in keeping with many of the parents' underplaying
of their role in the children's development to end this chapter with
quotations from the conversation of two mothers. The first, a mother
of four, all of whom were near the top of their class, including the
early fluent reader, and all of whom were knowledgeable and widely
read, commented, 'I think I've been very lucky with them all – I
didn't do that much.' Although she and her husband left school early
she added, 'They're going to get the chance. I'll see they take the
chance.' The second was one of a family of seven, who had also left
school early and who insisted that she was not well-educated and
was a bit of a 'duffer'. She commented, 'We would like to see them
making use of their life, doing something worthwhile, especially
when they have the chance – they're getting the chance nowadays.'
In these families both father and mother were interested and actively
involved in their children's education and concerned for their future.

CHAPTER IX

What Can We Learn?

Reading in a Language Context (Chapter I)

We are as far as ever from finding a single best method of teaching reading which will suit all teachers, all circumstances and all children (Chall 1967); indeed focus on this aspect of reading instruction has probably directed attention away from more important and rewarding aspects. The influence of the school situation and the ways in which the teacher is herself a variable affecting reading progress have been studied, her skills and her experience by Morris (1966), her language in early reading instruction by Reid (1966) and her sensitive observation of the children's responses by Clay (1972). Learning to read is frequently regarded as a sequential process developing from lower reading or decoding skills through intermediate or language related skills to higher or comprehension based skills, the latter being seen as characteristics of the skilled adult reader. The teacher concerned with the young child and the beginning reader has had her attention directed mainly, if not exclusively, to the lower decoding skills, with higher reading skills seen as a goal which her young charge will later, if successful, attain. She has tended to have too little appreciation of the effects that her initial approach to the reading situation may have on the children's later progress, on their motivation and appreciation of reading as a language based activity. She has also been too little aware of the complexity and range of skills that even the beginning reader brings to the reading situation. A range of language skills, an ability to anticipate probable sequences in print and an appreciation of the invariant nature of the 'read' as distinct from the 'told' story together with a high expectancy of interesting experiences from the printed word are all likely characteristics of the high progress child. The child who at first makes limited progress has indeed a number of relevant skills on which the teacher may not capitalize sufficiently; while her very language of instruction – or the material she uses – may be one cause of the failure which she attributes to the child. Studies of the child, his role in the learning situation and the characteristics he brings to the reading situation seem important; too much attention has perhaps been directed to those who fail or make slow progress with an analysis of their deficits which *may* in some instances have caused their failure. It is dangerous, however, to focus all one's attention on the failures and to assume that with the deficits which they exhibit failure was inevitable. This may be so, but one reason could be the expectation of failure which a variety of researches have set in the minds of the teachers. There is certainly evidence that teacher expectation influences the progress of the children. Goodacre (1968) has shown the lowered expectation which teachers tend to have for children from certain home backgrounds. It seems essential not to dismiss or explain away the instance which fails to fit our categorization or substantiate our theory (Bernstein 1973, p. 4). The exception is at least as important as the rule.

Recent researches have tended to emphasize the language context and its importance in the reading situation, not only the language of the teacher but the language of the text, and the significance of viewing reading as a 'psycholinguistic guessing game' (Goodman 1970). Although the importance of the phonic basis of the words is still stressed by many (Morris 1974), the importance of the linguistic structure of the text in which even the early reading material is embedded is also seen as important (Reid 1973). The importance of analysing even the beginning reader's response to print has been stressed with evidence of different patterns of miscues between high and low progress children (Clay 1969).

In a recently published book entitled *Help for the Reading Teacher; New Directions in Research* edited by Page (1975), the following points are stressed:

1. Understanding reading must be built on understanding what happens when the reader is interacting with written language.
2. Reading is a receptive language process which must be studied using the insights from linguistic research.
3. The reading process may be the same for everyone but each pupil learns to control it individually.
4. . . . even abnormalities must be considered in a framework of how meaning is constructed from written language
and finally:
5. Full appreciation of reading as the receptive phase of communication between the writer and reader means awareness of the extent to which the specific conceptual background and interest of the reader influences comprehension. (Page 1975, p. 5)

Attention has been paid and is increasingly being directed to an analysis of what the skilled adult reader does in a variety of situations and what the beginning reader is trying to do (Smith 1971). Surprisingly little attention has been paid to the young child who reads early and fluently and to an analysis of the extent to which he already exhibits the characteristics of the skilled adult reader rather than those of a child, the extent to which he even at an early age is already capable of 'interacting with written language' and the extent to which his specific conceptual background and interest influence comprehension. Durkin's study of *Children Who Read Early* (1966) is frequently referred to but few quotations of its findings are actually given and little attention has been paid to its significance in terms of approaches to learning to read. Her findings of the home backgrounds of the children, the interest and involvement of the parents, the variety of their backgrounds and their children's continued success in school are all important. Though they may not indicate that more parents should be encouraged to teach their children to read early they may none the less have implications for the teaching of reading to other children. More recently King and Friesen (1972) in a further study of children who read early found similar results to those of Durkin. Krippner (1963) as a result of his case study of a young child of three who was already a fluent reader warned of the danger of predicting failure because of deficiencies on certain tests which were beginning to form part of reading readiness batteries, since failure rather than success might have been predicted for his fluent reader. Torrey (1973) in her case study of an early fluent reader, a coloured boy from a poor home, stressed the fact that this child read early and fluently without forsaking his local dialect which was still the appropriate means of communicating in his home. In the study reported in this present book there was a child whose failure, like that of Krippner's boy, some at risk registers might have predicted: difficult birth, early concussion, mixed-handedness – yet this child had a reading age of over eleven at under five years of age (see pp. 41–2). Another child in this study like that in Torrey's was able to read fluently and early without forsaking his local speech – and to develop appropriate written language while still retaining his own distinctive oral language in situations in which he felt it appropriate (see pp. 87–8). Many of the findings in this present study are in line with previous studies of children who read early; they amplify rather than contradict them.

Summary of Findings

Thirty-two children (twenty boys and twelve girls), referred shortly after commencing school as already reading fluently, were observed over a period of years. Their initial and later attainment and other characteristics were studied together with their early experiences and home background.

Attainment (Chapter II)

When first seen the children's reading attainment was already beyond that which defines children as 'at risk'. The range of reading attainment was from seven years six months to over eleven years of age. All read with understanding a variety of reading material as well as books – many reading non-fiction as well as fiction. Most were already able to spell at least simple regular words, they also knew when they were wrong and their errors were usually a good approximation to English. Most were also well above average in arithmetic – especially when the tasks were presented orally in problem form. Thus their attainment was not limited to the reading situation, on the contrary, most showed skills in a variety of language based situations.

Intelligence and Other Characteristics (Chapters III and IV)

As a group the children were above average in intelligence and some were exceedingly gifted though some were of average intelligence as measured by the tests. Their strengths tended to be in the verbal rather than non-verbal aspects of the tests. The issue was raised as to the extent to which their high level of functioning owed anything to the stimulating language environment in which they were developing and it was felt that it would be wrong to dismiss them as merely a group of unusually intelligent children and to attribute their precocious reading development to an innate potential (see pp. 23–5). Although the group scored high on a test of auditory discrimination a caution was sounded that their success might owe much to the language context of the task and that the failures of other children might well stem from lack of these skills rather than a weakness in auditory discrimination even of speech sounds (see pp. 34–5 and also Williams 1975).

On tasks involving visual discrimination, on the contrary, few of these children were above average; a finding which was felt to have implications for remediation of children with reading difficulties (see pp. 26–32).

Early Experiences and Home Background (Chapters V and VIII)

The children came from a variety of home backgrounds, some were from large families, others 'only' children. Some parents had higher education and were in professions, others had left school early and had no further training. All parents did, however, seem to value education and to wish for their children what they had themselves experienced – or what they had missed.

The mothers and those fathers who were interviewed clearly found their families both stimulating and absorbing while most of the fluent readers had available at some time pre-school an interested adult who talked to and listened to them. Few mothers were working at the time of the first interview and those who were even at the later interview tended to have selected occupations and hours which enabled them to be available to their families as much as possible. The children were, however, encouraged towards choice of reading material by their mothers most of whom themselves read widely.

The parents found it difficult to differentiate the early fluent reader from other members of the family, most of whom were also successful in school. The commonest characteristics to be mentioned were powers of concentration and a self-sufficiency which meant the child could enjoy the company of others but in its absence be content on his own, together with a raised sensitivity to new or unusual experiences. Few of the parents had consciously attempted to teach their children to read and indeed some were embarrassed at their children's early rapid progress. An interest in their children's progress coupled with encouragement of independence of choice was a feature of most of the homes. Extensive use of the local library as a source of reading material was encouraged by the parents initially but later sustained by the children themselves. A number of the fluent readers had available an interested adult with time to devote to them at the stage when they were interested in reading – either to read to them, talk with them, or answer their questions. Most of the children appeared to read silently either from the beginning or from an early stage which made it difficult for the parents to pinpoint exactly when they began to read. For some their initial interest was in print in their environment, including on television, rather than specifically in books.

School Progress and Later Development (Chapters VI and VII)

Reports from the school indicated that these fluent readers continued to show impressive attainment in reading, spelling and in written work. Examples of their written work were sent by some teachers as an indication of its quality. The children also appeared well adjusted to school and to be seen as generally acceptable to their classmates.

Diaries kept by the children indicated their range of reading while their other interests at the time of the school reports were studied in a further interview. The extent to which the local library was a regular and valuable source of reading material for most was apparent as was their breadth of interest and sense of fun.

What Can We Learn?

Although clearly these children and their families had many features about them which were unique; the study has, nevertheless, implications for teachers and others concerned with reading and related skills.

The important role played by the local library in catering for and in stimulating the interests of these children is certainly one striking feature of the study. For most of these children the stimulus to use the library came initially from the parents though it was clear that the children themselves later found it a valuable source of information and enjoyment. The findings with regard to accessibility of different types of reading material, layout, advice and flexibility of regulations all have implications for libraries concerning ways of ensuring that children with potential but without the continuing support of a kind available to most of these children have access to reading material to suit their developing interests. The role of the class and school library and the development of greater links between school and local library in order to provide wide enough resources is certainly an aspect worthy of further consideration. Just as some local libraries had regulations sufficiently flexible to enable them to cater for the interests of children such as these, so also some schools see their class libraries, their school libraries and the local library as all part of an integrated service catering for children's needs. Some schools do indeed have on short or extended loans volumes and materials from the local library or arrange visits to the local library as part of the school curriculum. We do perhaps tend to underestimate the potential of many children or stay too close within an age-related structure in considering their likely interests. This seems particularly true with boys, judging by the evidence of the interests of a number of the boys in this research. It may well be that the majority of the children who appear to value the local library and to use it extensively come from homes such as those described in this present study and it seems important to consider ways in which the local library and the school can attract young readers who are less fortunate than the families in this study and can also sustain their interest. Several new developments are relevant in this connection. In a number of nursery schools children are read stories, sometimes the same stories repeatedly at their own request thereby giving them access to reading material which they would not previously have experienced, and so helping towards a love of books and an awareness of the concepts of print. There is, however, evidence that many of the children who request stories most often or show interest in books in nursery school are the very children for whom the home is already providing a variety of book-related experiences (Lomax in press). Some nursery schools do also provide a lending library from which parents can borrow books to read to their children – either books available from the nursery school's own stock or on loan from the local library. Thereby parents are both encouraged and assisted to play an active part in developing their children's interests. The likelihood of a rewarding experience for both child and parent is increased by such schemes and it also results in a linking of home and nursery-school experiences when books are made available which the child already enjoys or is likely to appreciate. Repetition of the same story read to a child has many values, not least the sensitizing of the child to the features of book language which is probably a far more valuable preparation for school than any attempts at teaching the child phonics or even a basic sight vocabulary.

Another study where parents of children who do not attend nursery school are encouraged to visit the local primary school which their pre-school child will attend for a weekly group discussion with other parents and to borrow books which their child might enjoy being read, also fits into this aspect (Donachy in press). Such schemes have many advantages, including the fact that they may reach many parents who would be unlikely to bring their child regularly to a pre-school. The first parents to join such a scheme will be those already active and involved; parent recruitment will gradually enable such a scheme to reach parents less involved and less confident of their own skills. Parents may develop a more positive accepting attitude to school and this may lead later to valuable interactions when the pre-school child begins school, even possibly extending to other children in these same families. Some of these parents are thereby also helped to appreciate that they do have skills which are valuable to their children's progress and to be less fatalistic in their views on development. When one considers the diffidence with which many of the parents in this present study regarded their contribution to their children's progress how much more so is this true of other parents. Such a scheme whose focus is on encouraging the parents to interact with their children and to appreciate the valuable contribution they can make and are making also leads the teachers who become involved to see education as a partnership with even these parents, whom they previously saw as either lethargic or hostile, as active and indeed essential partners. The importance of such developments seems to be underlined by the findings in this study of the valuable contribution that the parents made and were still making to their children's development by their interest, their encouragement and their respect for education.

Many children will still come to school from homes where language is used mainly for control rather than for communication and active interaction. For them story reading and verbal interaction will be not only a valuable but an essential part of the process of learning to read, not only motivating them towards an expectation of enjoyment from spoken and written language but also an essential aspect of learning the characteristics of print.

The existence of children such as those in the present research must lead us to question to what extent and in what ways learning to read is a developmental process and whether there are essential sequential steps. It may be necessary to consider whether those steps which are frequently regarded as sequential are so only because of the structure within which we *teach* reading rather than the pattern within which children *learn* to read. Given the possibility of using a variety of syntactical, semantic and phonic cues in arriving at meaning from print, the same individual will use these differently at different stages in his development of reading skill but also according to the position of words in a sentence or the presence of words in a particular context. The earlier a word appears in a sentence or the greater its isolation from a familiar grammatical context the more necessary will be alternative cues. Where children read orally or try out aloud words which cause difficulty, it is possible to study their possible strategies for arriving at meaning; where, however, as with many of these children they read silently it is often difficult to discover the particular strategies they utilize. It is none the less dangerous to assume without firm evidence to support it that the way we teach is the way children learn.

Clearly these children were becoming successful not only in extracting meaning from print but also in predicting the likely sequences of letters in words leading to high progress in learning to spell. They were also becoming aware of the characteristics of written language leading to successful and appropriate production of written language themselves. It is all too easy to say they are rare or atypical or intelligent or from good homes and to claim that though interesting their development has no relevance for the busy class teacher faced with the child of average or below average intelligence from a poor home which supplies little interest or encouragement. There are children, however, who can learn to read without formal instruction or the use of simplified vocabulary-controlled texts designed specifically for teaching reading. Such progress was clearly the result of the characteristics of the particular child – his powers of concentration, his memory for sounds in sequence, his precocious language development and his motivation combined with or more accurately interacting with the encouragement, stimulation and accepting interest of an adult. That the attributes of the particular child were an important aspect of the situation is not denied but the crucial role of the environment, the experiences which the child obtained, their relevance to his interest and the readiness of the adults to encourage and to build upon these, should not be underestimated. It is pertinent that while the children in this study learned to read early and indeed before starting school, many of their siblings learned quickly and effortlessly within the school situation. It seems important to consider the contribution of *their* home experiences to their success also, though for some of them the school might well have accepted the full credit.

It seems important not to ignore the evidence of children such as these – and of their brothers and sisters and to appreciate that education neither begins at five years of age, nor at nine o'clock in the morning! We are all too ready to attribute the failures to the homes but to claim the entire success for the school and formal education. Any theory of reading is adequate only in as far as it takes account of children such as these. If we are to improve the teaching of reading and the related skills it seems important to consider reading in a language context – a context which includes both school and home.

APPENDIX A

Initial Parental Interview

The precise wording of the questions varied but the questions below indicate the range of topics covered and also the subsequent categorization.

'He' is used throughout this outline although the same questions were asked concerning boys and girls.

1. How long has he been reading in the way he does now? What was his age at that time?
2. What does he like to read at the moment?
   Fiction/Non-fiction/Adult books/Comics/Press/Everything/other (including puzzle books, poetry).
3. Where does he get his books?
   School library/public library/bought/'inherited'/other.
4. Does he belong to a library (other than a school library)? YES/NO
   (a) If so, when did he first join?
       Before 5 on parents' ticket/own ticket
   (b) How often does he go to the library?
       Weekly/fortnightly/monthly/occasionally.
   (c) Does he choose his own books, or get help?
       Chooses own/gets help/both.
5. Does anyone read to him now? YES/NO
   (a) If so, the same or different books?
   (b) Who reads to him?
       Mother/father/sibling/other/all.
6. What does he do if he comes to a word he does not know?
   Asks/sounds out/guesses/other.
7. Do you often suggest books he would enjoy, or does he enjoy choosing his own? (borrowing and buying).
8. How old was he when he first started to try and read?
   1–2 years of age/2–3 years/3–4 years/4–5 years.
9. At what age did he first show an interest in written words and numbers?
10. How did he first start to read?
    (a) By interest prompted by mother in flash cards or alphabet and sounds or word or alphabet games/by interest in observing a sibling or friend learning/by interest in mother or sibling reading aloud/no apparent interest as above but started on blackboard and letter sets or books or press, comics or signs or kitchen packages.

11. What were some of the things that interested him in learning to read? To gain information/to emulate siblings/to read posters, packets, etc./watching television/nothing specific.
12. What kind of materials did he use? Books/signs/papers.
13. Did you ever buy books you thought would help? YES/NO
    (a) What kind? Picture books/story books/primers/reading scheme/ other.
    (b) When was he first helped?
    (c) What form did the help take?
    (d) Who helped mostly? Mother/father/sibling/other.
    (e) How often did they help? Daily/weekly/at odd times/ when requested.
    (f) Was the help regular or irregular? More systematic/more casual/part of every-day life.
    (g) What kinds of help? Told words he asked/comprehension checked/pictures discussed.
14. Could he write or print when he first started school? YES/NO
    If YES, was it printing or writing?
    (a) At what age did he first show an interest in printing or writing?
    (b) At what age did he first write or print?
    (c) How did he start?
        Copying letters or words/writing name/taught at school/other.
    (d) What kind of materials were used?
        Paper and pencil/blackboard and chalks/plastic letters.
    (e) What kind of help was given?
        Shown how and hand held/errors corrected/encouragement only/ other.
    (f) Did he use capitals or lower case letters?
15. What kinds of activities did he seem to do well pre-school? Pencil and paper games and painting/reading/manipulative games/ sport and active games/imaginative.
16. When no other children were available, what did he do? Pencil and paper games and painting/reading/manipulative games/ sport and active games/imaginative.
17. With whom did he play mainly? Children of his own age/younger children/older children/siblings/ no one/other.
    (a) When playing with other children, what did they do? Pencil and paper games and painting/reading/manipulative games/sport and active games/imaginative.
    (b) Was he a leader or follower?
18. Did he prefer to spend his time with adults or children?
19. Did he go to nursery school or play group?
20. Have you read any books about teaching children to read? YES/NO
21. Do you feel his interest in reading was initiated by himself or that you encouraged him to make a start? By child/by parent.
22. How did the school react to the child's reading?

Told/not noticed and had to be told/pleased/indifferent/said it gave scope/said it did not.

23. How interested is he in school?
Extremely/adequately/sometimes/not.
(a) Is he having any particular problems?

24. Have any of your other children read before starting school? YES/NO

25. Are any of the younger children showing signs of early reading?

26. Did you or your husband read before starting school?

27. Do you feel you and your husband read more than average, average or less?
(a) What kinds of books do you like to read?

28. How old were you when this child was born?

29. How old were you when you left school?

30. How old was your husband on leaving school?

31. Did either you or your husband pass any public examinations?
Father: O Level/A Level or highers/trade/professional/
Mother: degree/none.

32. What is your husband's work?

33. What was your work when you left school?
(a) Did you work after marriage?

34. Have you worked since you had children? YES/NO
(a) If so, full-time/part-time/occasionally/no.
(b) Do you work now? Full-time/part-time/occasionally/no.
If not, do you plan to? YES/NO

35. Thinking of your family as a whole, do you feel that any of your children have a closer relationship than usual with you, your husband or any other adult?

36. Did this young fluent reader watch television before starting school? If so, how often? Seldom/very often/regularly/selectively/non-selectively.

37. Are you aware of anything he has learnt from television?

In addition to answering questions on the range of topics indicated above, the parent was asked questions on the following topics:
Pregnancy and birth – condition of baby at birth; early health; hospitalization.
Early functioning – walking; talking; age on sitting; smiling; use of hands; hearing; vision.
Laterality of child and parents.
Family learning and family health.
Emotional and social behaviour – sleep pattern; crying; nail biting; aggression; temper; fears; bed-wetting; wandering. Separation from mother and duration.
Also the parent was asked to complete Rutter Child Scale A.

APPENDIX B

School Report Forms

The following details were obtained from the school and in addition two teachers were asked to complete Rutter Child Scale B; the first teacher and the one who provided the following information:

For completion by Class Teacher

NAME OF CHILD................   DATE OF BIRTH ....

SCHOOL......................   AGE ....

CLASS ....   NAME OF TEACHER ....

No. of Boys in Class   No. of Girls in Class
Age range of class

Is this the class for his/her age group? YES/NO
Are there other classes at the same age level? YES/NO
If so are they all comparable in ability level? YES/NO
If not, please give details of level of his/her class in relation to others ....
Please rate his/her present level in comparison with the present class
(Please circle appropriate category)

Reading accuracy	very low/low/average/high/very high
Reading comprehension	very low/low/average/high/very high
Composition	very low/low/average/high/very high
Spelling	very low/low/average/high/very high
Arithmetic	very low/low/average/high/very high
Writing	very low/low/average/high/very high
Art	very low/low/average/high/very high
Handwork	very low/low/average/high/very high
Physical Education or games	very low/low/average/high/very high
Music	very low/low/average/high/very high

Any additional comments on any of the above............................
Is he/she a leader in class YES/NO
Is he/she accepted by the other children in class YES/NO
Additional comments on abilities or interests not covered above
If he/she is in class for his/her age – do you feel promotion to a higher class could be considered YES/NO
Comments ....

If he/she has already been promoted, do you feel this has caused any problems   YES/NO
Please give details ....
What types of reading appear to appeal to him/her.................
Do you have problems in providing reading materials to suit his/her interests? ....
Do you find he/she has good concentration or is easily distracted........
Has his/her mother written or discussed any problems with you   YES/NO
If so, please indicate frequency and problems..............
Has his/her father written or discussed any problems with you   YES/NO
If so, please indicate frequency and problems..............
ANY OTHER COMMENTS:
Please enclose samples of recent written work if possible.

Signature ....
Date ....

Thank you for your co-operation.

For completion by Head Teacher

NAME OF CHILD ....   DATE OF BIRTH...............

SCHOOL ....   AGE ....

CLASS ....
Is this the class for his/her age group   YES/NO
If he/she is in class for age:
   Has promotion ever been considered   YES/NO
   If so, what were the problems?
   If not, were there any *specific* reasons for not trying this? YES/NO
   Please state reasons.
If he/she is NOT in class for his/her age:
   When was he/she promoted?
   At what age?   From which class   to which
   Do you feel this caused any problems?   YES/NO
   Please state problems
Has the child's mother written or discussed any problems with you? YES/NO
   If so, how often?
   For what reason?
Has the child's father written or discussed any problems with you? YES/NO
   If so, how often?
   For what reason?
Any other comments.
   Thank you for your co-operation.

References

Belmont, I. and Birch, H. (1966) 'The intellectual profile of retarded readers', *Perceptual and Motor Skills*, vol. 22 pp. 787–816.

Bender, L. (1946) *Bender Visual Motor Gestalt Test*, distributed by the National Foundation for Educational Research, Slough.

Bernstein, B. (ed.) (1973) *Class Codes and Control Vol. 2. Applied Studies towards a Sociology of Language*, Routledge and Kegan Paul, London.

Blank, M. (1968) 'Cognitive Processes in Auditory Discrimination', *Child Development*, vol. 39 pp. 1091–1101.

Blank, M. (1970) 'Some Philosophical Influences underlying Pre-school Interventions for Disadvantaged Children', in F. Williams (ed.) *Language and Poverty*, Markham Pub. Co., Chicago, pp. 62–80.

Britton, J. (1975) 'Teaching Writing', in A. Davies (ed.), *Problems of Language and Learning*, Heinemann, London.

Broadhurst, A. and Phillips, C. J. (1969) 'Reliability and validity of the Bender Gestalt Test in a sample of British schoolchildren', *British Journal of Social and Clinical Psychology*, vol. 8 pp. 253–62.

Cazden, C. B. (1970) 'The Neglected Situation in Child Language Research and Education', in F. Williams (ed.) *Language and Poverty*, Markham Pub. Co., Chicago, pp. 81–101.

Chall, J. (1967) *Learning to Read: The Great Debate*, McGraw-Hill, New York.

Clark, M. M. (1970) *Reading Difficulties in Schools*, Penguin Papers in Education, Penguin, Harmondsworth.

Clark, M. M. (1974) *Teaching Left-handed Children*, 2nd edition, University of London Press, London.

Clay, M. M. (1969) 'Reading Errors and Self-Correction Behaviour', *British Journal of Educational Psychology*, vol. 39 pp. 47–56.

Clay, M. M. (1972) *Reading: The Patterning of Complex Behaviour*, Heinemann Educational, New Zealand.

Daniels, J. C. and Diack, H. (1958) *The Standard Reading Tests*, Chatto and Windus, London.

De Bono, E. (1972) *Children Solve Problems*, Penguin Education, Harmondsworth.

D.E.S. (1972) *Framework for Expansion*, H.M.S.O., London.

D.E.S. (1975) *A Language for Life*, H.M.S.O., London.

Deutsch, C. P. (1967) 'Auditory Discrimination and Learning: Social Factors', in M. Deutsch et al *The Disadvantaged Child*, Basic Books, Inc., New York, pp. 259–77.

Donachy, W. (in press) 'Parent Participation in Pre-School Education', *British Journal of Educational Psychology.*

Downing, J. (1969) 'How Children Think about Reading', *The Reading Teacher*, vol. 23 iii, pp. 217–30.

Durkin, D. (1966) *Children Who Read Early*, Teacher's College Press, New York.

Goodacre, E. J. (1968) *Teachers and their Pupil's Home Background*, National Foundation for Educational Research, Slough.

Goodman, K. S. (1970) 'Reading: a psycholinguistic guessing game', in H. Singer and R. B. Ruddell (eds.) *Theoretical Models and Processes of Reading*, International Reading Association, Newark,. Delaware.

Hardy, M. I. (1973) 'The Development of Beginning Reading Skills: Recent Findings', in M. M. Clark and A. Milne (eds.) *Reading and Related Skills*, Ward Lock Educational, London, pp. 46–56.

Hunt, J. McV. (1961) *Intelligence and Experience*, The Ronald Press, New York.

Hutt, C. (1972) 'Sex differences in Human Development', *Human Development*, vol. 15 pp. 153–170.

Hutt, C. and Bhavnani, R. (1972) 'Predictions from Play', *Nature*, vol. 237, No. 5351 pp. 171–2.

Kellmer Pringle, M. L., (1970) *Able Misfits: The educational behaviour difficulties of intelligent children*, Longman, London.

King, E. M. and Friesen, D. T. (1972) 'Children who read in Kindergarten', *The Alberta Journal of Educational Research*, vol. xviii, No. 3, Sept., pp. 147–161.

Kirk, S. A., McCarthy, J. J. and Kirk, W. D. (1968) *Illinois Test of Psycholinguistic Abilities*, Examiner's Manual for the Revised Edition, University of Illinois, Urbana.

Koppitz, E. M. (1964) *The Bender Gestalt Test for Young Children*, Grune and Stratton, New York.

Krippner, S. (1963) 'The Boy who Read at Eighteen Months', *Exceptional Children*, vol. 30 pp. 105–109.

Lomax, C. (unpublished) 'Activities at Home and at Nursery School: A Study of Children showing high and low interest in Books and Stories at Nursery School'.

McCarthy, J. J. and Kirk, S. A. (1961) *Illinois Test of Psycholinguistic Abilities*, experimental edition, Institute for Research on Exceptional Children, University of Illinois.

McInnes, J. A. (1973) 'Language Pre-requisites for Reading', in M. M. Clark and A. Milne (eds.) *Reading and Related Skills*, Ward Lock Educational, London, pp. 100–104.

Maxwell, J. (1974) 'Towards a definition of reading', *Reading*, vol. 8, No. 2 pp. 5–12.

Morris, J. M. (1966) *Standards and Progress in Reading*, National Foundation for Educational Research, Slough.

Morris, J. M. (1973) 'You Can't Teach What You Don't Know', in M. M. Clark and A. Milne (eds.) *Reading and Related Skills*, Ward Lock Educational, London, pp. 105–112.

Morris, J. M. (1974) *Language in Action*, Resource Book, Macmillan Education, London.

Naidoo, S. (1972) *Specific Dyslexia*, Pitman, London.

Neale, M. D. (1966) *Neale Analysis of Reading Ability*, Macmillan, London.

Page, W. D. (ed.) (1975) *Help for the Reading Teacher: New Directions in Research*, National Conference on Research in English Bulletin Series; Eric Clearinghouse on Reading and Communication Skills, Urbana, U.S.A.

Paraskevopoulos, J. N. and Kirk, S. A. (1969) *The Development and Psychometric Characteristics of the Revised Illinois Test of Psycholinguistic Abilities*, University of Illinois Press, Urbana.

Pearce, J. (1972) 'Literacy is not Enough', *Cambridge Journal of Education*, vol. 2, No. 3 pp. 150–160.

Peters, M. L. (1970) *Success in Spelling*, Cambridge Institute of Education, Cambridge, England.

Reid, J. (1966) 'Learning to think about Reading', *Educational Research* vol. 9, No. 1 pp. 56–62.

Reid, J. and Low, J. (1973) *The Written Word*, Teacher's Manual for Link-up, Holmes McDougall, Edinburgh.

Rutter, M., Tizard, J. and Whitmore, K. (1970) *Education, Health and Behaviour*, Longman, London.

Schonell, F. J. and Schonell, F. E. (1960) *Diagnostic and Attainment Testing*, 4th edition, Oliver and Boyd.

Scottish Council for Research in Education (1967) *The Scottish Standardisation of W.I.S.C.*, University of London Press, London.

Smith, F. (1971) *Understanding Reading*, Holt Rinehart & Winston, New York.

Smith, F. (ed.) (1973) *Psycholinguistics and Reading*, Holt Rinehart & Winston, New York.

Stanley, J. C. (ed.) (1973) *Compensatory Education for Children ages 2–8: Recent studies of Educational Intervention*, Johns Hopkins University Press, Baltimore.

Start, K. B. and Wells, B. K. (1972) *The Trend of Reading Standards*, National Foundation for Educational Research in England and Wales, Slough.

Templin, M. C. (1957) *Certain Language Skills in Children*, The University of Minnesota Press, Minneapolis.

Terman, L. M. et al (1925 *Mental and Physical Traits) of a Thousand Gifted Children*, Stanford University Press, California.

Terman, L. M. and Merrill, M. A. (1961) *Stanford-Binet Intelligence Scale*, Manual for the 3rd Revision, Form L–M, Harrap, London.

Torrey, J. W. (1973) 'Learning to Read without a Teacher in F. Smith (ed.) *Psycholinguistics and Reading*, Holt Rinehart & Winston, New York, pp. 147–157.

Tough, J. (1973a) 'The Language of Young Children: the Implications for the Education of the Young Disadvantaged Child', in M. Chazan (ed.) *Education in the Early Years*, Faculty of Education, University College of Swansea, pp. 60–76.

Tough, J. (1973b) *Focus on Meaning: Talking to some purpose with young children*, Allen and Unwin, London.

Wechsler, D. (1949) *Wechsler Intelligence Scale for Children*, Psychological Corporation, New York.

Wechsler, D. (1963) *Wechsler Pre-School and Primary Scale for Intelligence*, Psychological Corporation, New York.

Wepman, J. M. (1958) *Auditory Discrimination Test*, distributed by the National Foundation for Educational Research, Slough.

Williams, P. E. (1975) 'Auditory Discrimination: Difference versus Deficits', in W. D. Page (ed.) *Help for the Reading Teacher*, National Conference on Research in English, pp. 91–100.

Zigler, E. and Butterfield, E. C. (1968) 'Motivational aspects of changes in IQ test performance of culturally deprived nursery school children', *Child Development*, vol. 39 pp. 1–14.

Index of Subjects

Index of Names